pocket guides

MONEY BOXES

by

Constance E. King

Series Editor: Noël Riley

LUTTERWORTH PRESS
Guildford, Surrey

First published 1983

Cover illustration shows the 'Frog and Snake'
tinplate bank, *c.* 1925. Photo: Messrs. Sotheby's.

ISBN 0–7188–2539–X

Printed in Great Britain by
Mackays of Chatham Ltd

Contents

Three of the most popular types of money boxes: a cast iron 'Jolly Nigger', a Staffordshire pottery cottage and a traditional 'piggy bank'. Private collection.

Introduction

FEW collecting fields offer the enthusiast examples made from such a diversity of materials as that of money boxes, and although the earliest specimens were discovered in the remains of Greek and Roman civilization, they have continued to be produced throughout the centuries, so that their appeal is easy to appreciate. Whether individual taste inclines towards ceramics, metalware, celluloid or other forms of plastic, there is an abundance of interesting examples to be discovered. The very wide price range is also attractive, and while even a child could afford to collect pieces made in the last thirty years, at the other extreme fine ceramic examples or the rarest of mechanical banks often form a sound financial investment. While in the 19th century the child was encouraged to save small coins for future prosperity, the inflation-educated infant of today would be far better advised to invest in the money boxes themselves.

The majority of adults possessed a money box in their childhood, and this has led many people to start a collection when they have discovered a familiar example in an antique shop or market and recalled the excitement of opening the box to purchase some longed-for toy. It is upon such children's boxes that modern collectors concentrate, but many were also made, particularly in the 19th century, for poorer adults, whose only chance of purchasing some small extravagance was to save over a long period. In the early 20th century, despite the number of Post Office savings accounts and other more secure means of protecting savings, small amounts continued to be kept in money boxes, silver threepences and sixpences in particular being accumulated in the small cylindrical chrome pocket versions with notches cut in the sides so that the saving could be seen at a glance. The money box, throughout its history, is therefore an object of dual intention, seen in its most colourful versions as a toy but also intended either as a functional or decorative piece for adult use.

Ceramic money boxes were collected with enthusiasm from the beginning of the 20th century, the main emphasis being upon the colourful products of the Staffordshire potteries, but it was in America in the 1920s that the money box began to attract a much wider following. These new enthusiasts specialized in examples made much more recently and included many of the amusing mechanical toys that were still in commercial production. Because some of the earliest American examples were in the form of actual buildings, the money box became known as a 'bank' or 'penny bank', terms that are now frequently used in Europe, as much of the language of this collecting area has originated in the United States. These collectors divided the money boxes into specific categories so that a 'still bank' is one that has no moving parts, such as a ceramic cottage, a pig or metal pillar box, while in contrast a 'mechanical bank' has moving parts and is usually made of metal, perhaps in the form of a man who shoots a coin into a tree trunk or a clown who runs in circles.

The 'registering banks' are perhaps less generally attractive but no doubt originally had greater appeal for the dedicated saver, as a mechanism recorded the total amount deposited. The enthusiasm of the bank collectors, combined with the substantial prices they were willing to pay, soon encouraged the manufacture of reproductions, some of which are so good that only the most experienced collectors can immediately detect them. The early Staffordshire cottage boxes have also been reproduced for many years, so that anyone wishing to invest seriously in this area is best advised to buy only from reputable specialists.

1.   Ceramic Money Boxes

SIMPLE hand-shaped or wheel-turned money boxes are found among the artefacts of early civilizations and although an individual maker might have added some incised decoration or introduced a different colour with a slip pattern, there was little variety in the basic utilitarian shape until the 18th century. A late 16th century reference describes a 'Box of potters clay wherein boyes put their money to keepe, such as they have in the shops towards Christmas', suggesting that, even in a period when Christmas presents were not often bought for children, the money box, with its connotations of thrift and personal discipline, was already an established favourite (fig. 1). The development of

1. An unusual pair of Dutch delftware money boxes made in the third quarter of the eighteenth century. The slots are in the dogs' backs. Height 8¼ in. Sold in October 1981 for £300.

2. and 3. The Staffordshire dog also enjoys a long history as a still bank. The larger example is decorated in brown and white. Both *c.*1880. The smaller 3½ in. high.

4. A Staffordshire earthenware cottage decorated in red, green and white with the slot in the roof. *C.*1855. Height 3½ in.

more colourful containers began with the production of delftware, such as that made at Lambeth from the 1670s, though examples from this period are extremely rare. The general improvement in life style and the increased interest of parents in their children's upbringing encouraged the manufacturers to produce more interesting shapes, such as a leaf-decorated salt-glazed stoneware bank made in Derbyshire in the early 19th century. This money box was obviously designed with some thought and with the intention of producing an object that would look effective on a table or mantlepiece and was the forerunner of the many colourful banks that were made in England. A large number of these earthenware boxes was created for the amusement of adults and formed an interesting household decoration. The increase in prosperity in the 19th century meant that ordinary working people could afford small ornaments for their homes and the Staffordshire potters were skilled in producing cheap but colourful pieces that would catch the eye (figs. 2 and 3). Virtually the same designs, with only minimal

5. *(left)* 'Anne Hathaway's Cottage', a glazed earthenware box with the slot in the roof. No access. *C.* 1910. Height 4½ in. 6. *(right)* A glazed earthenware 'Shakespere Saving Bank' with the slot at the back of the roof. Height 4½ in.

adaptation, were used for both pastille burners and money boxes, though the latter, which had to be smashed to obtain the contents, have survived in much lower numbers (fig. 4). The larger cottages, with an abundance of applied decoration and gilding, were fairly obviously made for adult use and have a lasting appeal because of the amount of fanciful detail that was added to fairly simple basic shapes (figs. 5 and 6).

In the last quarter of the 19th century, such traditional ornaments were replaced by even cheaper German ceramic versions, often in the form of whimsical animals or a sentimental portrayal of a group of children. These money boxes were produced in great number in Thuringia, alongside thousands of other novelty items, but as they were even more fragile than the earthenware, relatively few have survived in perfect condition. As with all ceramic banks, those that can be positively attributed to a particular maker are most desirable, those that are unmarked having to be valued according to the interest of their decoration and their basic quality.

7. *(below)* An unusual salt-glazed stoneware money box with titled busts of Queen Victoria, the Duchess of Kent, and allegorical Putti. Inscribed Turner Wilson 1838. Height 4½ in.

8. A Macedonian terracotta fruit with a slot but no means of access. Mid-19th century. Height 3 in.

Some of the most collectable English boxes are those produced by the firm of Doulton, founded in 1815 in a small pottery at Lambeth that was already manufacturing salt-glazed stoneware (fig. 7). One particularly fine example of the firm's early work took the form of a pair of Georgian town houses with bow windows on the ground floor and a dividing coach entrance. This salt-glazed stoneware model involved a great deal of skilled work and was probably intended for adult rather than child use. The slot was cut in the roof and as there was no other means of removing the money, surviving examples are extremely rare. Doulton showed much less interest in these ephemeral items during the second half of the 19th century, but in 1920 an interesting, yet much more crudely designed, bank was made for Kenneth Gordon Doulton. It represented an idealized Tudor cottage and was decorated at Lambeth in the strong colours often found on their well-known art pottery.

Many other china factories produced still banks, particularly in the form of animals or figures, but they usually formed part of the cheapest range, for sale at fairs and gift shops, and were frequently unmarked, so that they have to be individually valued and assessed

9. A ceramic still bank in the form of a London souvenir teapot. Polychrome decoration. C.1930, height 2½ in.

10. and 11. The ceramic piggy bank has long been the most popular form of money box. The marbled example *(left)* is marked 'Made in Austria'. The other, with slipware decoration, is unmarked. Both *c.* 1930.

(figs. 8 and 9). Of particular interest are the products of the various Arts and Crafts movements that arose from a desire to escape from the vulgar machine-made artefacts that were crowding homes in the second half of the 19th century. Money boxes were occasionally produced for the children of these parents of more aesthetic taste and often suggest a date much earlier than that of their manufacture. Perhaps the most amusing were those produced in a curious pseudo-antique manner by the eccentric Edward Bingham at his small factory in Castle Hedingham in Essex. Bingham often adapted designs he had seen in illustrations and museums in a delightfully abandoned way, so that despite an uninhibited use of clay and colour, the items have a primitive appeal that is popular today.

Despite the obvious charm of ceramic money boxes, the relatively small number to have survived means that there is only limited scope for an impressive collection and consequently the number of enthusiasts is comparatively low. In this century, many china factories have produced attractive specimens, some as souvenirs of particular events and

12. An earthenware 'Pin Money' box with transfer decoration and a generous use of gold lustre on the clasp. The crossed pins have bead heads. Supplied *c.* 1920 by a London store. Width 5½ in.

11

13. and 14. Two ceramic banks from the Royal Doulton 'Bunnykins' range. These newly issued pieces represent a football and a book.

15. *(below)* A brown and white stoneware bank representing Winston Churchill. Unmarked, height 4 in.

others as display pieces (figs. 10–15). Many craftsmen today also make exciting work well suited for the collector who has the good sense to realize that fine pieces are still being produced. Anyone wishing to purchase antique ceramic examples should search not so much through the stock of toy dealers but in that of ceramic specialists; similarly at auction, they are more likely to appear in the various china sales than in those devoted to toys.

2. Wooden Money Boxes

WOOD was the most obvious material for the construction of a small box, being strong yet capable of a great variety of carved or applied finishes. Although examples of very early ceramic banks have survived, wood, being less able to withstand damp, rotted and fragmented, so that although it seems highly likely that they must have been used from the beginning of civilization, examples are not known. The splendid caskets with painted decoration or ironwork embellishing and strengthening the surface that were used to keep valuables out of the hands of servants are not included within the collector's definition, as the piece must have a slot for a coin and must also be of household use rather than public designation. This definition excludes, for instance, the very decorative church offertory boxes. The plainest wooden boxes (fig. 16) were often made more attractive with colourful painted patterns which usually give an indication of the

16. A beechwood example with an interior divider. Simple but well-made boxes such as this remained popular throughout the 19th century. Width 6 in.

country or region of origin (fig. 17). Wooden still banks continue to be relatively cheap, as the plainer versions have less visual appeal than those with complex mechanisms, though some of those produced by skilled cabinet-makers with precisely inlaid brass embellishments can be of the very highest quality. As with ceramic banks, they are more likely to be found in general antique shops than among the stock of toy specialists, and the simplest examples, such as those of pine or matchboard, decorated with a glued-on photograph or lithographed pattern can be most satisfactorily light on the purse (fig. 18). The quality of wooden money boxes varies more than any others, the type of craftsmanship, the style of decoration and the country of origin all having to be taken into account.

Some of the most desirable wooden boxes

17. A turned wooden box with the slot in the lid, decorated in green and red. South German or Swiss. *C.*1900, height 5 in.

18. A commercially made wooden bank, decorated with a coloured lithograph in Kate Greenaway style and ornamented with lead edgings.

are those decorated with the mosaic-like patterns in various woods, known as Tunbridge ware. Similar mosaic work was also made in the mid-19th century in Italy though, in general, this Sorrento work relies on a variety of dyed woods, making it more colourful than mosaic ware made in England. Visitors to the spa of Tunbridge Wells looked for attractive gifts to take home and money boxes featured alongside the snuff and trinket boxes. Probably because so many were given to children, the survival rate of banks in comparison with other wares like needlework accessories, is low, making any example a most desirable acquisition. One of the most appreciated is an extremely rare dial-operated sovereign box whose top was decorated with typical Tunbridge mosaic. The sides were composed of a series of horizontal rows of letters and the container could only be opened when the word 'Surrey' was brought into alignment. This particular example can be seen in Birmingham Museum, and it is likely that others were produced for different counties or towns.

Other Tunbridge ware money boxes were veneered with satin or holly wood and then inlaid or painted with scenes or designs. The characteristic shiny surface was achieved either by painting or varnishing. The earlier pieces are comparatively simple but during the 1850s many of the designs were based on the patterns for Berlin wool work. The very complicated mosaic work was not individually pieced together on each box but was assembled from lengths of natural and coloured woods between six and twelve inches long that were carefully arranged in the desired patterns and then glued together. Very thin slices were cut and used for the sides and tops of the boxes, being set into rosewood, bird's-eye maple or boxwood. This skill was often developed in families over several generations so that a very high degree of sophistication was attained. After varnishing or polishing, the surface was completely smooth.

More crudely made marquetry money boxes were created in other parts of Europe and, during the last quarter of the century, this craft became popular with adults who were inspired by the designs suggested in craft books and magazine articles. These home produced boxes have to be judged purely on the quality of the work, though those with local

19. A tartan ware boxwood still bank with a printed view of 'The New Post Office, Ipswich'. There is a flap in the base for access. Width 4 in.

interest, or those commemorating specific events or decorated in high art noveau or art deco style will obviously command a much higher price. The well made but plain box, perhaps decorated only with the owner's name has, in comparison, a very limited appeal.

The organic curves of patterns in the art nouveau style were particularly suited to pyrography, commonly known as poker-work, a technique embraced by amateur craftsmen in the late 19th century, though its origin was ancient. Designs for the decoration of poker-work money boxes appeared in many girls' and ladies' magazines but as the technique was often used on cheap, flimsy wood, the number of surviving examples is surprisingly low. Some of the most beautiful pieces of this work were made by professionals who used sophisticated equipment with platinum-pointed pokers heated by gas or electric furnaces, some of the most highly stylized examples originating in Germany. As with the inlaid versions, poker-work boxes have to be judged individually, though they are not very popular and their price is usually low. The majority are of the simplest box shape with a lock and key, but as so many were sold by craft shops for home decoration there is usually little variety in the basic shapes.

Similar plain wooden money boxes could be ornamented in a variety of ways by the small fancy-goods supplier or home craftsman and identical boxes are often found embellished with shells, coloured stones, beads, barbola work or applied lithographed paper. Such work can be extremely attractive when carried out with skill, but despite the hours of patient work often expended, its financial value today is very low and effective examples can be found for as little as £2–£4.

The so-called tartan ware is, in comparison, much more generally collected, as a number of fine pieces were made mainly for adult appreciation. The manufacture of Scottish souvenir woodware developed from the making of decorated snuff boxes and reached its peak in the

20. A wooden barrel with a printed view of the Pavilion Hotel, Folkestone. The box is a press fit with the slot on top. Height 4 in.

21. A boxwood still bank with a view of St Nicholas Church, Guildford. It has a side flap for access. Width 3 in.

mid-19th century. The box tops were decorated with transfer applied prints and the sides with colourful tartans. During the 1820s these sides were painted but as this was obviously very time consuming, it was replaced around 1850 with printed paper. The application of the tartan paper was a highly skilled technique and it is often difficult to see the paper at all, as the edges of the boxes were first painted black so that the pattern blended into the surface. The later money boxes in this technique have photographs or lithographed scenes or incidents and are again especially desirable if they are commemorative in character. The Scottish firms produced a quantity of this work for sale in Europe, so that it is not unusual to find a

German scene surrounded with Scottish tartan (figs. 19–22).

Instructions for the manufacture of money boxes were almost invariably included in the 'do-it-yourself' books that were published in ever increasing numbers after 1870. Money boxes were ideal as small gifts or as items for sale at fairs and bazaars, though a few that incorporated some form of mechanism were quite complex. One design, in *Amateur Work Illustrated*, was for a windmill whose sails turned twelve times when money was dropped into a slot, an effect achieved by a clock mechanism. In another version two dancing Negroes were set in motion when the coin fell. Similar designs, such as a boat tossing on the waves, were offered in different publications, but almost all made use of clock mechanisms. In the hands of a skilful painter and carver these wooden mechanical banks were highly effective but when a poor amateur's work was combined with the suggested inscription:

'I'm ready and willing to take a spin,
   If you are as willing, to drop a penny in.'
The result was to give the home-made mechanical bank the very shortest of lives.

The introduction of fretwork as a popular craft in the late 19th century made it possible for the home worker to produce much more sophisticated effects, as it was only necessary to purchase sheets of patterns. The fretwork money boxes are sometimes lined with wood of a contrasting colour or sometimes coloured card was applied to the inner surface so that the curves and detail of the decoration stood out effectively. The majority of the designs were for simple casket shapes, but some more ambitious projects were also suggested such as the 'Automatic Calendar Money Box' included in *Hobbies Magazine* with the maxim in 1937 'Resolve to use it every day and acquire the thrift habit at the same time.' The publisher was able to supply the mahogany and plywood for this safe-like construction. Much more attractive was the 'Scot Money Box' that

22. A boxwood bank with a printed view of the New Tay Viaduct. Marked 'Made in Germany'. Height 4 in.

No. 1887 THE "SCOT" MONEY BOX
8 ins. long.

A coin laid on the tray tilts the figure and is automatically deposited in the slot of the box.

Fretwood and Fittings—A parcel of Whitewood, with Brass Padlock, Key, Catch with Hasp complete, and pair of Hinges, for 2/- ; post free 2/6.

23. The 'Scot' money box designed for fretworkers and advertised in *Hobbies* magazine in 1937.

represented a Scottish boy who dropped a penny into a house when a coin was placed on his tray-like hand (fig. 23). It was difficult even for a professional to make a mechanical wooden bank that was really effective and it was only with the advent of metal as a generally used material for toys that boxes could be made in really alluring variety.

3. Mechanical Banks

IT is to America that the collector looks when thinking of metal money boxes. The social reasons for their popularity can never be fully accounted for, though the explanation must be partly in the attention paid to the inculcation of good habits. Children were trained to observe the basic conventions, and lying, cheating and the spreading of slander were all punished with great severity. Saving and the discipline of mind involved in putting aside a little money each week were also made a feature of childhood. For the American settlers, battling to establish civilization, money was without the taint of vulgarity with which it was regarded by educated Europeans, so the bank became a symbol of steady progress and made an excellent child's gift combining virtue, ambition and thrift.

As the rigid discipline that governed life in the 18th century was relaxed, books and toys as well as money boxes became more suited to the needs of the child, and the simply made boxes of the previous century were soon replaced by banks that put some enjoyment into saving, as the child watched an animal or

24. A cast iron 'Mule and Stable' bank. The coin placed between the hind legs of the mule is tossed into the stable as a dog appears causing the mule to buck. The base stamped 'Pat'd Aug. 3rd 1880'. Length 8¾ in. Sold for £130 in May 1979.

25. In this frog cast iron bank a coin placed on the stomach of a small frog is kicked into the mouth of a larger frog when a lever at the rear is pressed. The base stamped 'Pat'd Feb. 2 1875'. American, late 19th century. Sold for £220 in May 1979.

26. A cast iron bank in the form of a squirrel and nut. A coin placed on the front paws is deposited in the tree trunk when the lever at the base is pressed. American, late 19th century. Length 7 in. Sold for £220 in December 1978.

figure perform some amusing action (figs. 24–28). These mechanical banks were made in great variety and formed a significant section of the stock of every shop or mail order firm. The continuing American affection for banks is now reflected more in the number of collectors than by their place in the toy departments. Because of the competition among American collectors it is in the U.S.A. that the really high prices for unusual banks are seen, whereas in Europe quite a rare piece can pass through a saleroom at a low figure, as can be seen by the prices realized for some of the boxes illustrated.

During the 18th and early 19th centuries American boxes followed the traditional patterns of those found in Europe and were only given individuality by some painted decoration or inlay. However, by the 1850s American banks began to develop a character of their own, as much more extensive use was made of metal. There had been some manufacture of tinware and pewter toys in the late 18th century, forming the earliest traceable development of the native toy industry. The earliest pieces were made by local tinsmiths and given only minimal decoration. They are difficult to identify, as local craftsmen continued to work in the traditions of their original countries. The tin toy industry developed rapidly after 1840, but though savings banks were made, they are not easy to find as tin bent easily and damaged boxes were soon discarded. Some of these early examples took the form of houses, bandboxes or churches and were decorated with very thin paint and finished by stencilling, lettering or lining.

27. A cast iron 'Lion and Monkey' bank by Kyser & Rex. The monkey on the tree throws a coin to the lion which opens and shuts its mouth when a lever is pressed. The second monkey was missing in this example. Sold for £90, December 1978.

28. *(left)* The 'Hoop-La' cast iron bank in which a dog leaps through a hoop to deposit a coin in the barrel. Lever operated. By John Harper & Co., English, early 20th century. Length 8½ in. Sold for £95 in July 1980. 29. *(right)* A cast iron 'Speaking Dog'. The coin, placed on the tray, is deposited in the bank as the girl's other hand moves. The dog opens his mouth and wags his tail. Made by Shephard Hardware and J & E Stevens Co. Late 19th century, width 7¾ in. This example, with the base cracked, sold for £100 in July 1980.

30. A card-playing Chinaman in cast iron, made by J & E Stevens Co. The coin slot is beneath the left hand. When a lever is depressed the Chinaman moves the left hand to reveal the spread cards and raises his right hand to his face. Originally designed by James H. Bowen. This example was not in working order. Length 8 in. Carries English and American patent dates. Sold for £500 in May 1981.

31. An American mechanical bank with a cashier at the door. The coin is placed on the cashier's tray and when a lever at the side is depressed the door swings inwards. Patented in 1873 and 1876 by H. W. Prouty. Manufactured by J & E Stevens Co. Length 4¾ in.

The first chartered savings banks were opened in the U.S.A. in 1816, and this early date, far in advance of the British Penny Bank introduced in 1850, no doubt further encouraged the American interest in thrift. The most splendid boxes developed from the use of cast iron as a toymaking material, particularly in the 1870s and 1880s. The earliest were frequently based on substantial buildings with Georgian style windows and pillared façades: in heavy letters over the door the child could read 'Savings Bank'. One of the first patents for a mechanical movement was filed in 1869 for 'Halls Excelsior' and its novelty value obviously encouraged other designers. Enthusiasts estimate that one firm alone issued around four hundred different types working on systems of levers, cogs, springs and wheels that are sometimes highly complex. One of the most prolific makers was J. & E. Stevens of Cromwell, Connecticut, established in 1843 who, in their 1873 catalogue illustrated some twenty-four different models (figs. 29–33). Some, such as the 'Cat and Mouse Bank' seem to have been designed more as ornaments than playthings as the model resembles an ornate mantle clock with the cat in low relief on the clock face. This bank was patented by James Bowen for J. & E. Stevens (fig. 34). In a very rare version the cat, holding the mouse in its

mouth, is made of brass but this was soon replaced by iron, making the earlier version
much more desirable for the collector. An ad-
vertisement for this bank advised the buyer to:

'Place a coin in front of the mouse over the
cat, press the lever, and as the coin dis-
appears into the bank, the kitten in fancy
dress appears, turning a somersault, holding the mouse and ball.'

These iron American banks were cast by
hand and made by pouring molten metal into
a sand mould, which accounted for the slightly
rough texture of some of the models (fig. 35).
Many of the designs remained popular for a
long period and despite their early appearance
were still in commercial production in the 20th
century. The range of subject matter was
great; in 'Jonah and the Whale', Jonah
reaches out to place the money in the mouth of
the whale who then appears to swallow it. The
'Trick Dog' jumps through a hoop when a coin
is placed in his mouth and deposits the offering in a barrel. 'Punch and Judy Bank', 'Trick
Pony' and the 'Artillery Bank' all operated in
a similar manner, the coin being placed on
some sort of platform and shot into the container (figs. 36–46). Some money boxes such
as the 'Circus Elephant' or the 'Dark Town

32. An 'Eagle and Eaglets'
bank by J & E Stevens Co.
The mother bird drops a
coin into the fledglings' nest
when a lever is pressed.
The base stamped 'Pat'd
Jan 23 1883', 8 in. long.

33. In this cast iron bank
made by J & E Stevens Co.,
coins placed in the jockey's
mouth are dropped into a
coin slot in the base when a
lever is depressed causing
the mule to buck and throw
the jockey. The base is
stamped 'I always did
'spise a mule'. Length 10
in. Late 19th century.

34. *(above left)* A 'Cat and Mouse' bank with a lever pivoting device. On one side is a running mouse and on the other a cat and mouse. American, late 19th century. Height 8½ in. Sold for £95 in December 1977.   35. *(above right)* A cast iron 'Boy on the Trapeze'. A coin placed on the boy's head causes him to revolve and deposit it in the pierced base. Probably by J. Barton Smith Co., Philadelphia. Late 19th century. Height 9½ in. This example with some rust sold for £100 in May 1980.   36. *(below left)* A cast iron 'Trick Dog' bank in which the small dog leaps through the hoop to deposit a coin in the barrel when a lever is pressed. Marked 'Pat. July 31 1888'. Length 8½ in. Late 19th century, sold for £120 in May 1979.   37. *(below right)* In this cast iron 'Punch and Judy' bank Judy deposits the coin when Punch beats her. American, late 19th century. Height 8½ in. Sold for £150 in December 1977.

Battery', that represents three Negroes play-ing baseball, are even more complex but all were manufactured with a great awareness of the need for strength in a toy of this type and have stood years of use with an ease that must upset many modern toy makers.

Louis Hertz, a very long-established auth-ority on American toys, comments that fake banks of the mechanical type began to be made in the 1930s and quotes the 'Carnival Bank' which apparently surpassed many genuine products in its degree of complexity. The maker used a Stevens coin trap and made up patterns and castings so that to all intents and purposes a virtually genuine bank was produced. This money box, of which only six appear to have been made, was based on a try-your-strength type of machine in which a figure struck down with a mallet, forcing a coin upwards, inside a pole, until it rang a bell at the top. This bank is a curious example of a fake that is now collectable in its own right.

Many of the other banks continued in pro-duction over a long period, using identical parts and paints, so a late example that has been subjected to wear can look deceptively old, a characteristic that encouraged the

38. A 'Trick Pony' cast iron bank by Shephard Hardware Co. The pony drops a coin into the manger when a lever is pulled causing the head to drop forward. Stamped on base 'Pat'd June 2nd and July 7th 1885'. Width 7½ in. Sold for £120 in December 1978.

39. In the cast iron 'Artillery Bank' the mortar fires coins into a brick bunker. The base is marked 'Pat'd May 1892'. C.1900, width 8 in. Sold for £85 in May 1979.

40. *(right)* The 'Dark Town Battery', cast iron bank by James H. Bowen. The coin in the bowler's hand is thrown towards the striker when a lever at the side is depressed. The base was repainted in this example. American, late 19th century. Sold for £140 in December 1978.

41. *(below right)* The 'William Tell' cast iron mechanical bank, the base stamped 'Patented June 23rd 1896'. The coin placed on the gun knocks the apple off the boy's head when the man's right foot is pressed. Length 10½ in. Sold for £200 in May 1980.

42. *(below)* An 'Elephant and Three Clowns on the Tub'. A coin placed between the rings held by the arms of one clown is deposited in the tub by the swinging trunk of the elephant when the ball held on the feet of another clown is pulled and released. Patented August 8th 1882 by J & E Stevens Co.

manufacture of so many fakes in the 1970s. These reproduction banks were usually sold quite legitimately by the manufacturers but in the hands of unscrupulous dealers and collectors, were often 'aged' with abrasives such as sand. These now appear so frequently in antique shops and auction rooms and cause such uncertainty among collectors that they have depressed the value of the genuine examples. The antique-buying public obviously likes to acquire an object that is both unusual and eye-catching but once reproductions of such pieces can be seen in hundreds in every gift shop, the genuine loses its attractiveness except to the most dedicated enthusiasts.

The Society of the Mechanical Bank Collectors of America numbers many passionate enthusiasts among its members and uses as its symbol one of the most complex banks ever produced, the 'Girl Skipping Rope' in which a somewhat elderly looking child, wearing a short skirt and a blouse with a frilled collar, is suspended on a bar, the metal 'rope' swinging around her most realistically when the dropping coin sets the mechanism in motion. To her right stands the money container, ornamented with leaves, scrolls and a squirrel, in high Victorian style. This famous money box, like many other first-class pieces, was made by J. & E. Stevens' Manufactory, though it was

43. *(above)* An 'Elephant and Howdah' cast iron box by Enterprise Manufacturing Co. The elephant swallows the coin placed in his mouth and a wooden figure appears from the howdah when a lever in the rear is pressed. American, late 19th century. Length 6½ in. Sold for £150 in December 1978.

44. *(centre)* One of the more common American banks is the 'Creedmore' in which a soldier shoots a coin placed on his gun into the tree stump when his right foot is pressed. Late 19th century. Length 9½ in. Sold for £20 in May 1979.

45. *(left)* An American cast iron bank marked on the base 'Pat. Pendg & Pat'd Feb 2nd 1875'. The lever on the base releases the spring on the gun so that the coin shoots into the bear. Height 8 in.

46. The 'Leap Frog Bank' by Shephard Hardware Co. The figure leaps over his partner's back to place a coin in the tree stump when the lever is pressed. Width 7½ in. Sold for £220 in December 1978.

47. A Monkey Barrel Organ cast iron bank. The monkey raises his cap and tips a coin placed on his tray into the organ. The motion is activated by a handle at the side that also works a simple musical movement. Marked 'Pat'd May 31st 1881'. American. Late 19th century. Sold for £220 in December 1978.

designed and patented by J. H. Bowen of Philadelphia in 1890.

One of the most attractive American mechanical banks is 'Little Red Riding Hood', who sits at the foot of a bed talking to her pale faced grandmother. When a coin is deposited the face drops away to reveal the wicked wolf below. 'The Lady Columbine' is another money box that has an almost universal appeal, partly because of the complexity of its structure; it represents a lady dancing around harlequin and a clown, and was first manufactured around 1906. In the 'Organ Bank' a monkey doffs his hat when a coin is put on to his plate and he then drops the money into the container in the body of the organ. This bank is particularly attractive as it also contains a crank-operated musical box in the base, giving it a dual appeal (fig. 47).

Among the most frequently reproduced banks are 'Jonah and the Whale' and the 'Dentist and Patient' though by far the greatest number are made in imitation of the Negro who swallows a penny, a bank that even originally was manufactured in huge numbers and over a very long period. This was one of the few mechanical banks to become really popular in Britain and few children born before 1930 could have been unfamiliar with this toy (figs. 48, 49 and 50).

The mechanical banks that most attracted

48. *(left)* The most common of the cast iron banks was the so-called 'Jolly Nigger'. This example was sold with two others for £60 in August 1977. American, early 20th century. Height 7 in.   49. *(centre)* 'The Young Nigger' bank, though a little more unusual, does not command a very high price. This example was sold with two others for £60 in August 1977.   50. *(right)* 'Dinah' the female version of 'The Jolly Nigger' is modelled with more detail. This 7 in. example sold with two others for £85 in August 1977.

51. In the 'Uncle Sam' cast iron mechanical bank by Shephard Hardware Co., the figure drops coins into his bag and opens his mouth when the lever at the side is pressed. Late 19th century, height 11½ in. Sold for £140 in October 1981.

the early collectors were those with complex mechanisms or those representing famous events (fig. 51). Stevens produced a particularly ugly caricature of Gen. Benjamin F. Butler who was represented as a green-backed frog whose mouth gaped to receive coins. This bank was made as a parody of Butler's advocacy of the issue of vast quantities of paper money in an attempt to relieve debts after the Panic of 1873. Butler was a member of the Greenback Party and stood as Presidential candidate in 1884. The American public, acutely conscious of the value of a sound currency, distrusted Butler and he is represented in the bank with one arm bearing the inscription 'Bonds and Yachts for me' and the other, 'For the Masses', while in this hand he carried a wad of paper money marked $1,000,000.

A Stevens money box, issued in 1873, parodied the Tammany Hall swindle that had shocked America. This showed a plump, well-dressed gentleman, representing William Marcy Tweed, sitting in an armchair and nodding his thanks when a deposit was made. Tammany Hall was the headquarters of the controlling organization of the Democratic Party of New York City and State, and Tweed and his party of politicians had swindled the city out of millions of dollars. The Tammany bank, like several others of topical interest, was still in production some forty years after the event, though it had by then become known as 'The Fat Man's Bank' (fig. 52).

The evolution of American mechanical banks is now usually traced from the patent issued in March 1876 to Charles C. Johnson for a bank building with two doors. On a platform outside stands a cashier with a coin tray. After winding the clockwork mechanism, the money is placed on the tray, an activating lever pressed, and the figure moves along a circular slot to the left door. He leaves the money in the bank before re-appearing from the right door to await the next deposit. A later version, made by H. L. Judd of Wallingford, Connecticut, replaced the cashier with a dog carrying a

52. In the 'Tammany Bank' a coin placed in the right hand is deposited in the left hand pocket while the head nods. Marked 'Pat'd June 8 1875'.

plate in his mouth. The later version was also crank rather than clockwork operated. Several of the mechanical banks were originally produced with clockwork mechanisms and these are obviously the most coveted by collectors as they are rarer.

Apart from the study of patent registrations, one of the best sources of information on the development of banks is in the pages of the mail order catalogues that were a feature of 19th and early 20th American life. The annual catalogues from Schwarz, the New York toy

53. An American 'Cabin bank' in which the Negro turns a somersault and deposits a coin placed on his feet into the roof when a whitewash brush at one side is moved. The base marked 'Pat'd June 3rd 1885'. Length 4½ in. Sold for £110 in October 1981.

shop, form a particularly useful record of the popularity of various types. Their 1886 pages offered a range of banks, mostly of the still or registering type but including an 'Uncle Tom Iron Bank'.

The catalogue states:

'This is a comical and amusing bank; by pressing a button at the back of neck the eyes roll up and the tongue is thrust out for a coin which when placed upon it is drawn in and deposited in the vault.'

In this version 'Uncle Tom' was embossed on the Negro's collar. The 'Iron Organ Bank' was much more complex and received the following description: 'Large chime of bells, dancing figures revolve when the handle is turned, the monkey deposits the coin in the vault and politely raises his hat.' The company added that this particular bank was too heavy to be sent by post.

It is very noticeable that by 1892 the popularity of mechanical banks was much increased and that the weight of these iron pieces no longer seemed to present any mailing problems as they were packed in stout wooden boxes. The 'Monkey Organ Bank' was obviously still a great favourite but there was also a more interesting 'Cabin Bank' with a Negro standing at the door and the accompanying instructions to 'Place the coin upon the roof above the negro's head, move the handle of the white-wash brush and the negro will be made to stand on his head and kick the coin into the bank' (fig. 53). Even more enticing was 'Professor Pug Frog's Great Bicycle Feat'. As the crank was turned and a lever pressed, 'Professor Pug Frog performs his great bicycle feat and the coin placed on the bicycle is deposited in the bank. During the performance Mother Goose gives attention to

54. One of the most decorative of printed tinplate banks is the 'Royal Trick' elephant who swallows coins placed in his mouth when the tail is pulled. In this example the tail is missing. German c. 1920. Sold for £450 in December 1978.

Place
coin
Here

Put a coin in the slot, then you'll see something funny,
Press my tail hard and I'll swallow the money.

her melodies'. The 'Eagle Bank' also remained popular for many years and represented a somewhat evil looking mother eagle in whose beak the coin was placed. After the lever was pressed, the eaglets rose from their nest, crying for food. As the eagle bent forward to feed her young the coin fell into the money container. In 1892 an improvement on the 'Monkey Organ Bank' was marketed 'With new dancing figures standing on either side of the monkey which revolved as the money deposited the coin from the tambourine in which it was placed, into the bank'. The 'Cat and Mouse Bank' already mentioned was also offered in this catalogue and described as being handsomely ornamented in fancy colours.

55. In the 'Frog and Snake' tinplate bank the frog opens its mouth to take a coin from the snake when a lever is pressed. German, c. 1925. Length 6½ in. Sold for £2,000 in December 1978.

56. *(left)* A Mickey Mouse tinplate mechanical bank. The figure rolls his eyes and the tongue protrudes to receive a coin when his ear is depressed. The reverse shows Mickey with a camera entitled 'Smile Please' and the rhyme:

If you only pull my ear, You will see my tongue appear,
Place a coin upon my tongue, Save your money while you're young.'

Marked 'By exclusive arrangement with The Ideal Films Ltd. All rights reserved. Registered No. 508041.' Probably of German manufacture. Sold for £750 in February 1980.

57. *(centre)* A German printed tinplate bank with the inscription:

Press the lever lightly, Watch my tongue appear,
Save a penny nightly, Make your fortune here.

The coin is swallowed by the Negro. *C.*1920, sold for £140 in September 1979.

58. *(right)* A German printed tinplate money box with a 10-pfennig slot and a pull-down lever operating two total dials in pfennigs and marks. Decorated with figures of children. Height 5 in. Sold for £90 in September 1979.

Tinplate Mechanical Banks. Printed tinplate banks, though they seem fragile were often surprisingly sturdy and still function well. Many, especially those made in the 20th century, carry their registered design and patent numbers, which make identification possible and add to their attractiveness to collectors. Though only few 19th century examples appear on the market a great variety was made in the second quarter of this century and

59. A printed tinplate money box representing a dog kennel. When a cord is pulled the dog retreats into the kennel with the coin in his mouth. The door then closes. Height 4½ in.

60. *(left)* A tinplate amusement machine bank with a coin slot at the side. The top section is glazed. British, made by Crescent Toys. The back stamped 'DGMT Ltd. Crescent'. Height 6 in.

61. *(right)* A printed tinplate 'Jumping Frog' bank. The frog leaps up the ladder when a knob at the side is pressed. Height 5 in., *c.* 1950. This was sold together with the Crescent amusement machine for £28 in December 1978.

62. An English tinplate mechanical bank. When the window slide is moved a coin tray appears by the rabbits and the woman looks upwards. Height 4 in.

range from animated nursery scenes to pin ball games. By far the most popular and expensive are those based on the Walt Disney characters, especially Mickey Mouse. The majority of the more interesting were made in Germany but in the 1930s British and American firms became more competitive and a number of very austere versions appeared. Though these are often mechanically interesting, they have only limited appeal, the enthusiasts preferring such examples as a dog which emerges from a kennel or a bank in the form of an animated shop scene, as it is the interest of the surface decoration rather than the basic construction that usually commands attention. (Figs. 54–66.)

63. *(above left)* A musical tinplate safe bank. The wooden knob at the front turns pointers that indicate European capitals on one side and figures on the other, accompanied by a tune. The windows indicate figures. Height 4 in.

64. *(above right)* A printed tinplate bank in the form of a house with a sliding window which reveals a counter with a cashier. Probably German, *c.*1935.

65. *(below left)* A tinplate mechanical bank: a sailor with articulated arms and a lever which, when pressed down, causes him to stand at attention and salute. Height 6½ in. German, *c.*1925–30. Sold for £160 in May 1980.

66. *(below right)* A printed tinplate mechanical 'Punch and Judy' bank with characters fighting on stage. English, *c.*1930.

67. A printed tinplate
vending bank for dispensing
'Chocolat Menier'. The
coin slot is in the lid above
a hexagonal column, with a
glass window and a drawer
at the front. German,
*c.*1920. Sold for £30 in
December 1978.

BANKS that dispensed a small sweet or chocolate when a coin was deposited are known as vending banks and form a most attractive collecting area within the sphere of mechanical banks. As these toys were originally intended for the 'sale' of confectionery they often took the form of a small street kiosk or are almost miniature versions of the large vending machines that stood in public places before the last war (figs. 67, 68 and 69). Though they are now avidly collected in America they were originally made in the greatest number in Germany and, to a lesser extent, in France. Although their exteriors vary considerably, both with regard to colouring and shape, their principle remains the same, the coin engaging the release mechanism so that a drawer could be opened to release the sweet. The money was retrieved and the contents replenished by opening a panel at the back or side with a key. The child was consequently given great encouragement to save by the reward of a sweet. Most of these banks carry advertisements for specific brands such as Pascalls, Droste or Stollwerck Brothers. Many are extremely attractive, almost in the manner of fairground decoration, with colourfully lithographed patterns on every available surface. Some were produced in distinctive versions for different countries but others included advertisements in English, French and German on the same box, giving an unusually international effect for the period. When in good condition such banks are very effective and it is little wonder that they form one of the more expensive areas of bank collecting.

68. *(above)* A tinplate, red-painted chocolate vending bank, probably of British manufacture. Height 6 in.

69. *(below)* A printed tinplate vending bank that released sweet cigarettes. Height 6 in. Sold for £40 in January 1979.

Register Banks

70. An attractive brass
house with glazed windows
and carrying handles.
There are two dials for
totalling the contents.
American, *c.* 1900. Height
8 in.

ALONGSIDE the highly ornamental
mechanical banks, completely functional devices were produced that
registered the amount that the saver deposited
(figs. 70, 71). Some of the registering banks
took the form of a shop till and obviously
appealed to children of both sexes. Certain
designs remained popular for a long period.
For example 'Uncle Sam's Three Coin Register Bank' was manufactured over fifty years
with very little change of design from when it
first appeared in 1912. The cash register banks
seem to have held greater appeal for European
children as they formed such ideal accessories
for model shops, though again the Americans
produced the greatest variety. Such banks
seem to have reached the height of their popularity just before the First World War, when
they could be obtained in cold-rolled steel with

gilt decoration, black japanned with gilt lettering or in black enamelled steel. All registered the amount deposited and a bell rang as in a genuine shop till.

It is very noticeable that in British and European catalogues from the turn of the century, money boxes play only a small part and were not provided with special sections as in the American publications. Some of the banks in Gamages 1913 catalogue are very much in the American idiom, such as a:

'Sixpenny register bank. Made from cold-rolled steel, securely riveted, forming a closed deposit vault in which the mechanism is securely placed away from meddlesome fingers, money can be taken out when 100 deposits have been made when figures will read (000), at which point coins are shaken out through a slot at the back of the bank, holding it upside down and pressing and holding the lever down. The bank is finished in black japan enamel, beautifully ornamented and everlasting. When coin is inserted in front of bank, marked "d" press lever down, which rings bell and deposit is registered and amount shown on the indicator, be sure and register each coin before depositing another, use only one coin at a time. If you need money before the bank contains 100 deposits use an axe.'

71. The 'Codey Magic Money Box', a registering bank that opened when 30 pennies had been saved. Unmarked.

6.

Safes

72. The splendid effect of the American safe-type banks is exemplified by this intricately cast model, the 'Fidelity Trust Vaults'. It has a clever opening device in the form of a clock face allowing the safe to be opened at 1.50. On the other sides are characters in niches, 'paying teller' and 'cashier'. Height 6½ in., late 19th century.

THOUGH banks in the form of safes are not as decorative as, for instance, the cast iron mechanicals, they were sometimes made more attractive by coloured lines and ornamental detail (fig. 72). In 1886 Schwarz were offering a combination safe as 'Something quite new and hardly a toy. Impossible to open it unless you have the combination. A good large substantial bank in every particular.' In 'Watch Dog Safe', among the most effective of its type, a dog barked when a deposit was made. In complete contrast 'Security Safe' was made of oak and was finished 'In black japan, relieved with different shades of bronze'. Another safe, measuring a mere 6 in. high, was described as 'Burglar proof' because of its combination lock capable of nine hundred changes. The 'Boudoir Combination Lock Safe', designed to resemble a handsomely bound book, was obviously intended for much wider family use as it contained several divisions and a drawer and was described as useful for keeping household valuables.

Some of these nickel-plated safes were originally quite handsome in appearance, with their coppered combination locks and gold-bronze decoration. Details such as massive embossed hinges and inset panels combined to give the money box an impressive air of solidity. 'The Bank of Columbia' was constructed on the lines of an actual safe with the dials and a handle on one side and Uncle Sam and Liberty on the others. In 1914 a steel combination safe of very advanced design with black japanned finish and lithographed doors was offered alongside more romantic models representing caskets or bound books.

Some banks do not fit precisely into either category: the 'Fortune Teller Savings Bank' worked on a similar principle to the registering banks but instead of indicating the amount deposited it revolved a wheel that told fortunes.

'Its mystery facinates and no one can withstand the temptation of dropping another nickel into the slot. It simply coaxes the coins out of everybody's pocket into the capacious vault and enriches the owner of this wonderful savings bank beyond expectations.'

Both registering banks and safes, though sold in Europe, were never as popular as in America and comparatively few designs are available in contrast to the great variety offered to American children.

7.   Still Banks

THE simplest money boxes, furnished only with a slot for the coins, are termed still banks (figs. 73, 74). This is a collecting area that was ignored until comparatively recently. During the last ten years enthusiasts, especially in Europe, have looked again at the very great variety of shapes and designs available and, realizing that the finest mechanical examples have been purchased by the Americans some years ago, have decided to concentrate on new areas. The most popular category is inevitably metal and includes those of cast iron, tinplate and the various cast alloys that were ideal for representing delicate

73. *(left)* A well made mahogony money box with a brass plate inscribed 'Percy. 23rd June 1877'. The leather guards inside the slot prevented the money being removed with a knife. English, width 6¾ in.

74. *(right)* A bronzed 'Post Office Savings Bank G.R.' with the stamped number 128703. The small savers could accumulate coins in these boxes which could only be opened at the Post Office. Similar boxes were also issued by several banks. *C.*1912, width 4 in. Sold for £18 in October 1981.

75. An ornamental cast iron still bank representing a mountain chalet and made in America in the late 19th century. Height 7 in. Sold in May 1979 for £40.

effects such as the features of a popular character or the texture of an animal's hair.

The cast alloy or cast iron banks were usually made in two sections bolted together and then given a lacquered finish in bronze or aluminium; others were cast in one-piece moulds in white metal, a technique that was preferred in Europe. These cast metal still banks are not yet sufficiently expensive to attract the makers of reproductions, so interesting collections can still be formed without the novice having to worry too much about fakes. Some collectors specialize in dogs or lions or those representing political characters, and others in buildings. These are a good collecting field, for despite their small size, it is surprising to see how much detail they incorporate. A 7½ in. 'Palace Bank' included gables, a tower, a *piano nobile* and some twenty-two windows. The 'Sky-scraper bank',

76. A brass money box in the form of a bank inset with a clock face. American, *c.* 1900. Height 10 in.

77 and 78. *(above)* Two cast iron still banks representing the Blackpool Tower. The larger is 7 in. high. *C*.1910.

79. *(below left)* A robust cast still bank of Mickey Mouse with red gloves, red shoes, and yellow shorts. Height 8½ in. Sold for £50 in February 1980.

80. *(below right)* Surely one of the smallest cast iron still banks is this American building measuring only 2¼ in. high.

81. An unusual hollow cast lead still bank of a Negro baby made in the early 20th century when dolls of this type were a novelty.

82. A small tinplate red fire bucket that is key-locked on the base. *C.* 1935, height 3½ in.

finished with a gold-bronze roof and towers, green-bronze door trimmings and aluminium bronze base, had an astonishing five hundred open windows despite its height of a mere 6½ inches. One of the smallest still banks in the form of a building stands only 2¼ in. high (figs. 75–80). Some of the buildings were made of more expensive metals such as brass and make extremely attractive display items, often originally purchased to give a glint of warm colour to a cottage mantlepiece rather than as a repository for a child's savings.

Indisputably of nursery intention were the lighter banks in cast metal such as 'Mary and her Lamb', representing a prettily dressed

83 and 84. A pair of English advertising still banks, *(left)* the tin-can version promoting salmon and *(right)* the small house Sharp's Toffees. *C.* 1930.

long-haired child standing alongside a lamb into whose back the coin was dropped. The 'St. Bernard Bank' was suggested as an ornamental as well as a toy product in 1903, as was a 'Magnificent Indian head finished in copper gold and bronze and is a work of art that will attract attention anywhere'. Formidable standing Indians, rabbits, boy scouts, teddy bears and pigs all made suitable subjects for cast metal still banks. During the First World War a particularly fierce bulldog wearing a soldier's cap was made to encourage war savings but others in the form of hats, birds, dolls and toys such as golliwogs continued in production until the 1940s, when metal was replaced by hard plastics for the majority of boxes. The metal still banks have to be valued according to the interest of the subject and the skill of manufacture so that items of a commemorative nature or in the form of an item in a popular toy collecting field such as character baby dolls or bears will arouse much more interest than a simple pillar box or coffer. Among the more collectable of metal banks are those that were originally made to contain biscuits or sweets and served as advertising items as well as toys (figs. 81–85).

In the area of printed tin the interests of two groups of collectors again converge, so that prices are higher. Direct printing on to tin-plate began in Europe in 1855 and a few money boxes were made in this early period though mass production really began in the 1860s and 70s with various forms of transfer printing. Colour printing directly on the surface of the tin was very difficult as the smooth, shiny surface could not take a direct print from a block or printing stone, a problem that was

85. A printed tinplate still bank marked on the base 'Model of the Queen's Dolls house. Issued by Chubb & Sons Lock and Safe Co. Ltd. 128 Queen Victoria Street, London, E.C.4. By special permission of Her Majesty the Queen (and with the consent of Cauldon Potteries Ltd) One shilling each. The Queens Charities benefit by the sale of each model. A diminutive Chubb safe protects the Queen's Dolls Jewels.' A flap in the base has a key. *C.* 1924. £23.

86. Printed tinplate books have remained a popular form. This example 'Dignity and Impudence' is key-locked. Height 7 in.

solved in the 1870s by the evolution of various methods of printing the design on paper and then transferring it from this more sympathetic substance to the tin itself. In the field of decorative prints France was the leader and supplied many of the sheets used by the box makers of other countries. A whole variety of patents for improvements in the different techniques was recorded in the second half of the century and the tins of this period are remarkable for their richness of colour and generous use of decoration. The advent of offset lithography, developed in Britain by Barclay & Fry, meant that the complete printing could be carried out on the press itself, the image being picked up on a glazed cardboard impression cylinder and then immediately stamped on to the sheet tinplate. This method was patented in 1875. It meant that highly decorated tins could be produced cheaply and toymakers were quick to take advantage of a material capable of so many differing effects. Some of the finest examples were made up from ten different colours as well as lacquers and gold sheens, giving a richness of effect that would be much too expensive to emulate today. As the many colours and varnishes used on a single sheet soon lost their elasticity if left, the stamping out into shapes and the assembly of the banks had to be carried out with great speed (figs. 86, 87 and 88).

The tinplate money box that has continued in production for the longest period is the well-known pillar box, the earliest examples bearing Queen Victoria's cypher. Some of these most basic of money boxes have lift-off lids, but more frequently the money has to be retrieved by shaking the coins through the slot or lifting them out on a knife, which soon damaged the container, so early examples are not

87. A printed tinplate still bank of a sentry box made *c.* 1920. It had a removable lid.

88. 'Ye Curiosity Shoppe', a painted and gilded tinplate still bank made around 1965 in response to the growing public interest in antiques.

easy to find. The pillar boxes were sometimes given additional detail such as children playing, or a printed figure posting a letter (figs. 89, 90).

The most collectable of tin money boxes are those issued as advertisements by biscuit, confectionery and tobacco companies, though it is often impossible to know the actual manufacturers of the boxes themselves, as too often it was only the name of the maker of the contents that appeared. One of the few known makers was Barclay & Fry, who began their manufacture of tin in the 1890s and included a splendid lighthouse money box made for W. Dunmore & Son among their first products. This bank, very unusual in that it carries the maker's name, represents the golden coloured stonework of an idealized lighthouse with printed figures standing on the steps and looking over the rails. The slot was situated on the tiled roof section that lifted off completely. The child must have derived pleasure from the fact that after the contents were consumed they would still be left with an attractive toy.

A very popular tinplate money box is that known as the 'Dolls House'. It represents a simple family house with a light covering of snow and a postman delivering the mail. This box has a rather roughly cut slot on the roof and was used by Mackenzie, the Edinburgh biscuit maker. Another version, without the slot, was used by Peek, Frean and C.W.S., and enthusiasts believe that the cutting of the slot to adapt the tin into a money box, for the Edinburgh firm, was a much later addition. The comfortable red brick house with its bay window is colourful and effective and engenders the sense of security which the accumulation of pennies was intended to give.

Another attractive house was used by Macfarlane, Lang & Co. and represented a traditional English cottage with a tiled roof. This is an unusual bank as the tin came apart at the sides, hardly a satisfactory arrangement when the bank was full. This 'Wonderland Cottage' was decorated with nursery rhyme characters

89. A pillar box marked 'Burnett Ltd. London'. It also bears a printed alphabet and pictures of the Bank of England, made *c.*1927.

including Little Red Riding Hood and Mary, Mary. On the reverse side Alice is seen at tea with the March Hare, the Dormouse and the Mad Hatter. This amusing tin was made just before the last war and is an indication of the way in which the basic house design, representing security, was continually improved and adapted.

One of the most prolific users of printed tin-plate boxes was the Reading biscuit maker,

90. This oval pillar box has two slots and on the back a print of Dick Whittington. It is stamped with the number 14777.

Huntley & Palmer. This firm included a vending bank among their still banks in the 1930s, a bank that differs completely from the Edwardian kiosks, as the design is so economical. The sides of the tin carried the instructions for operating, the child being told to use old pennies and that only the firm's 'Nice' biscuits would fit. The lower section contained a mechanism that released a biscuit for every coin deposited. Another very collectable Huntley & Palmer vending bank was produced around 1936 and represented a bob sleigh scene with an abundance of incident. The penny ran down a slide at the back to release the usual pull drawer. This firm also made extensive use of the simple pillar boxes, one of the more attractive showing children playing in the snow around the base. Much of the fascination of collecting advertising still banks is that new examples continually come to light, and though it is only possible to date pieces approximately, some firms, such as Huntley & Palmer, still have old catalogues and advertising material which facilitate dating. The costumes of the people are one of the surer methods of arriving at an approximate date, as the majority of companies would not wish their product to appear out of date. One effective bank, issued by Mackintosh Toffees, was in the form of a telephone kiosk on which was printed a young girl searching for a number in her notebook. This bank was doubly effective as at the side was a simple crank that rang a bell.

Among the most collected of advertising banks in Britain are those used by Crawford biscuits and especially those designed by Mabel Lucie Attwell. Her 'Bicky House', issued in 1933, was advertised as:

> 'A bright selection of biscuits of certain appeal to children specially designed by Mabel Lucie Attwell whose famous delineations of child life in pictures and postcards must have appealed both to children and parents for many years.'

Bicky House represented a rural cottage with a thatched roof, dormer windows and shutters. Around the door peeped the characteristic Attwell child.

'Fairy House' was issued in 1934 and took the shape of a toadstool, the stem forming a house with printed windows out of one of which a child gazed at a pixie pushing another fairy on a cart loaded with apples. 'Fairy Tree' issued in 1935 is perhaps the most memorable because of its long, cylindrical shape with a conical top on which, against dark leaves are seen the fairy folk. All these money boxes are charming, with their surfaces full of incident, while the basic construction was also skilful: the lower part of each tin contained the biscuits which were completely separated by a

57

91. *(above)* The well detailed 'Thermo X' gas fire money box that suited dolls' houses so well.

(below) The back of the 'Thermo X' fire made by John Wright & Co., Birmingham.

metal divider, allowing the coins to be collected before the contents were consumed.

The collecting of printed tins, neglected for decades, has recently become one of the largest growth areas among banks as interesting pieces can still be found. In America during the 1920s and 30s, a series of tin can banks, some 2 to 3 in. high, were given away as advertisements for tinned food of the same type. This was a particularly clever idea as the banks were identical to the full-sized tins but supplied with a slot cut in the top. The variety of these tin can banks is wide and though less decorative than the lavishly ornamented pieces used by the biscuit makers, are much collected and promote such products as 'Bab-o-cleanser' and 'Ocean Spray Cranberry Sauce'. Though such functional pieces have little appeal for toy collectors, the advertising enthusiasts find them attractive because of their almost ephemeral quality (fig. 91).

8.   Collecting

AS in any sphere of antique collecting, the beginner is advised to study the subject as widely as possible before spending high sums of money. Curiously, despite the fact that money boxes form such a popular collecting area, there is little published work on the subject, and nothing at all on banks except in America. Even there, where bank collecting is long established, literature is sparse, though occasional articles appear in collecting magazines. The new enthusiast is advised to research banks in specialist books on particular materials, so that ceramic boxes, for instance, will be found in works on Staffordshire wares and advertising banks in books on printed tins. There are also few specialist dealers in money boxes in Europe, the majority of boxes sold usually forming part of a more general stock of antique toys. Dealers are usually pleased to help collectors who seek advice on buying and developing a worthwhile collection, though they become understandably annoyed at the person who 'picks their brains' and then buys some inferior piece off a market stall. If a dealer is aware that a collector will buy from him over several years it is in his own interest to see that the quality of acquisitions is good. Obviously, as a collection improves, earlier purchases will be returned and swapped for finer pieces and the dealer will not want to be left with boxes that are inferior. The care for a good customer therefore becomes useful to both parties and until enough knowledge is gained to make purchases in the conviction of absolute authenticity and completeness it would be better to follow the dealer's advice.

In the area of still banks, the new collector is fairly safe, as the reproductions are obvious and sold legitimately as modern. The area of mechanical banks is, in comparison, much more dangerous and many general dealers actively avoid purchase, as they may have made quite expensive mistakes. This caution has actually depressed prices in this area, giving the European expert an occasional chance to buy a good piece at a comparatively low cost. The auction room prices provided in many of the photograph captions give some idea of how greatly prices in this field can vary. A bank that was considered rare three years ago might change its value completely if a number suddenly appeared on the market. Similarly, two collectors searching for a particular item can cause a sudden rise in price, making it essential for the collector to become familiar not only with current prices but also with the needs of his fellow enthusiasts.

Whether china, wood, tinplate (figs. 92 and 93) or even bakelite is chosen as a collecting field, buy only those pieces that are in really fine condition. Though many collectors work

92. The tinplate locking cash box remains one of the most popular designs. This English example is marked 'Chad Valley No 10016'.

93. A printed tinplate globe with a slot on the side. The complete model had to be unscrewed for access. German, c. 1925. Unmarked. Height 4½ in.

on the basis of selling or exchanging a less fine piece when they find the perfect example, this is not always possible, as in times of economic depression the growth of collecting areas declines and the new collectors, who would welcome the less perfect piece in better times, are not to be found, though the market for a bank in good condition is always there. The money box that can be positively dated, with a known maker, or with a commemorative or historical link obviously has more appeal than the nondescript though pretty piece. Again, as in any type of antique collecting, it is unwise to buy purely as an investment for, like stocks and shares, values rise and fall as different types of banks become popular and then decline. Such items are meant to be enjoyed and have to be valued according to the pleasure they give to the individual. When attending an auction, for instance, treat the catalogue with caution and study the piece yourself with care, noting any defects or imperfections and then decide exactly what the piece is worth to you. Then the dealer who scoffs because you overpaid will probably regret the piece in a few years' time when your taste was found to be well advised. All any collector can do, once he has studied his subject thoroughly is to back his own judgement and be prepared to forget bad mistakes. If complete security of investment is sought, then your money is better deposited in a full sized bank.

Books for Further Reading

The following publications contain sections on money boxes:

Franklin, M. J. *British Biscuit Tins, 1868–1939*, New Cavendish Books, 1979.
Griffith, David *Decorative Printed Tins*, Studio Vista, 1979.
Hertz, Louis H. *Mechanical Toy Banks*, Mark Haber, 1947.
—— *The Toy Collector*, Funk & Wagnalls, New York, 1969.
Hornung, Clarence P. *American Antiques*, Abrams, 1977.
Hutchison, G. A. (editor) *Indoor Games and Recreations*, Religious Tract Society, 1891.
Mace, L. H. & Co. *Toys*, 1907 Catalogue, New York.
Mosler, Edwin H. *The Encyclopedia of Collectables*, Time-Life Books.
Pinto, Edward H. & Eva, R. *Tunbridge and Scottish Souvenir Woodware*, G. Bell, 1970.

Magazines

Antique Toy World, 3941 Belle Plaine, Chicago, Ill. 60618, U.S.A. (bi-monthly).
International Toy and Doll Collector, P.O. Box 9, Halstead, Essex (bi-monthly).

Acknowledgements

The author and publishers would like to thank the following for permission to use the photographs in this book:

Antiques of Childhood 12, 17, 18, 19, 21, 21, 22, 74, 82, 85, 88, 89, 90; Bethnal Green Museum 43; Messrs. Christie's 31, 56, 58, 59, 69, 79; Stuart Cropper, London 80, 81, 83, 84, 87; Margaret Dell, London 16, 86, 92; Royal Doulton Tableware Ltd. 13, 14; Hobbies Magazine 23; Phillips Auctioneers 1; Pollock's Toy Museum 2, 3, 4, 5, 6, 8, 9, 10, 11, 15, 66, 68, 71, 77, 78, 91, 91A, 93; Messrs. Sotheby's 7, 24, 25, 26, 27, 28, 29, 30, 32, 33, 34, 35, 36, 37, 38, 40, 41, 42, 44, 45, 46, 47, 48, 49, 50, 51, 52, 53, 54, 55, 60, 61, 63, 64, 67, 70, 72, 75, 76.

Index

Bold page numbers refer to illustrations

INSIGHT GUIDES

GUERNSEY

POCKET GUIDE

◉ Walking Eye App

YOUR FREE EBOOK AVAILABLE THROUGH THE WALKING EYE APP

Your guide now includes a free eBook to your chosen destination,
for the same great price as before. Simply download the Walking Eye
App from the App Store or Google Play to access your free eBook.

HOW THE WALKING EYE APP WORKS

Through the Walking Eye App, you can purchase a range of eBooks and destination
content. However, when you buy this book, you can download the corresponding
eBook for free. Just see below in the grey panel where to find your free content and
then scan the QR code at the bottom of this page.

Destinations: Download essential destination
content featuring recommended sights and
attractions, restaurants, hotels and an A–Z of
practical information, all available for purchase.

Ships: Interested in ship reviews? Find inde-
pendent reviews of river and ocean ships in this
section, all available for purchase.

eBooks: You can download your free accompanying digital version of this guide here. You
will also find a whole range of other eBooks,
all available for purchase.

Free access to travel-related blog articles
about different destinations, updated on a
daily basis.

HOW THE EBOOKS WORK

The eBooks are provided in EPUB file format. Please note that you will need an eBook reader installed on your device to open the file. Many devices come with this as standard, but you may still need to install one manually from Google Play.

The eBook content is identical to the content in the printed guide.

HOW TO DOWNLOAD THE WALKING EYE APP

1. Download the Walking Eye App from the App Store or Google Play.
2. Open the app and select the scanning function from the main menu.
3. Scan the QR code on this page – you will then be asked a security question to verify ownership of the book.
4. Once this has been verified, you will see your eBook in the purchased ebook section, where you will be able to download it.

Other destination apps and eBooks are available for purchase separately or are free with the purchase of the Insight Guide book.

TOP 10 ATTRACTIONS

CASTLE CORNET
Step into the past at Guernsey's ancient royal fortress, standing guard over St Peter Port. See page 28.

ST PETER PORT
Explore Guernsey's endearingly quaint capital taking in the old town and colourful port. See page 25.

FORT GREY
Gripping stories of shipwrecks are the theme of the museum within the fort.

HAUTEVILLE HOUSE
Victor Hugo's home in exile shows that the French author was also an inspired interior

GERMAN OCCUPATION MUSEUM

Excellent war museum showing how the islanders lived during the Occupation. See page 46.

SAUSMAREZ MANOR

Historic family manor with delightful gardens, a fine sculpture park and visitor attractions. See page 38.

VAZON BAY

Ride the rollers or hire windsurf or paddleboard gear on this whopper of a sandy beach. See page 55.

ST ANNE, ALDERNEY

The island's capital is an engaging little town with cobbled streets and quirky shops. See page 78.

SHELL BEACH, HERM

This dazzling white beach is a paradise for shell collectors. See page 65.

SARK

Take a day trip to this tiny, car-free island and enjoy the walks and wildlife. See page 68.

A PERFECT DAY

9.00am

Breakfast

Christies in the heart of St Peter Port (43 Le Pollet, open from 8am and 9am Sun) offers a coffee-and-croissant fix or a full English breakfast. Watch the world go by or secure a seat on the balcony for lovely harbour views.

10.00am

Picture-postcard port

Explore the cobbled streets of St Peter Port, stroll along the waterfront to Cornet Castle or up to Hauteville House, where Victor Hugo penned *Les Misérables*.

Noon

Cliff walk

For views that inspired Impressionist painter, Renoir, take the first section of the south coast cliff path starting at South Esplanade in St Peter Port and ending at Fermain Bay, one of Guernsey's prettiest beaches. (Allow at least an hour as there are quite a few steps).

1.00pm

Lunch break

Fermain Beach Café has the best fresh crab sandwiches on the island and a lovely terrace on the beach. Alternatively, splash out and lunch at La Frégate (www.lafregatehotel. com) in St Peter Port, for Guernsey's best seafood and a terrace with a sublime view out to Herm and Sark – even as far as the coast of France on a clear day.

IN GUERNSEY

Vazon Bay
Further along the coast watch or join the surfers on the golden sands of Vazon Bay. Guernsey Surf School (www.guernseysurfschool.co.uk) hires out all the gear. Vistas Beach Café, right on the beach with a roof terrace, has great views.

10.00pm

On the town
RED, on the waterfront, has a cool cocktail bar (along with top-quality steaks); or for something more traditional try the Old Government House Hotel's Crown Club with its red leather seats and antique brass. Familiarly known as the OGH, and located up the hill from the main shopping street, this was the former residence of the governor of Guernsey.

6.00pm

Sunset cocktail
Continue along the coast to Cobo Bay and catch the last of the sun's rays on the spacious terrace of the Cobo Bay Hotel, a favourite spot for admiring the views.

3.00pm

West Coast
Head west to Rocquaine Bay where Fort Grey's Shipwreck Museum tells the grim story of vessels wrecked on the rock-strewn coasts. Portelet Harbour southwest of Fort Grey has a pretty sandy cove, ideal for a dip if the tide is out.

8.00pm

Dining options
Return to St Peter Port for the best choice of restaurants. Indulge in a slap-up seafood dinner at Le Nautique (see page 107), Mora (see page 106) or Pier 17 (see page 107), all with harbour views.

CONTENTS

INTRODUCTION

Sitting just off the Cherbourg peninsula, it is not surprising that Guernsey and its little sister islands have a heady mix of French and British cultures. Author Victor Hugo, exiled to Jersey and then to Guernsey, where he wrote *Les Misérables*, felt perfectly at home in the Channel Islands, describing them as 'morsels of France fallen into the sea and gathered by England'. It was this fusion of French and English culture, along with superb scenery and the sunniest location in the British Isles, that appealed to UK visitors in the early days of tourism. Although not truly British, the Channel Islands have been linked with the British Crown for over 900 years, the official language is English, cash machines dispense sterling and you drive on the left.

Guernsey may be the most densely populated of the Channel Islands but it retains quaint rural lanes, fine sandy beaches and miles of spectacular cliffs in the south. The island has one of the largest tidal movements in the world, with waters retreating twice a day to reveal large expanses of golden sands and lunar-like seascapes, pierced with rocks and reefs. Along with traditional beach pursuits such as swimming, windsurfing and rock-pooling, there has been a growth in adrenalin-fuelled activities such as sunset abseiling, cliff face rock-climbing or coasteering explorations.

Toads and Donkeys

Guernsey and Jersey run their affairs separately and there has been rivalry ever since they took opposing sides in the English Civil War. To this day, Jerseymen call Guernseymen *ânes* or donkeys while Guernseymen call Jerseymen *crapauds* or toads, there being no toads on Guernsey.

In the unlikely event you tire of the coast, Guernsey has monuments ranging from eerie Neolithic tombs to Napoleonic towers and World War II bunkers and tunnels – potent reminders that the Channel Islands were the only the parts of the British Isles occupied by German forces. The south of the island offers 28 miles (45km) of cliff-top walks; and the network of Green Lanes, where traffic is restricted to 15mph

Sark's rocky coastline

(24kmh), was developed with walkers and cyclists in mind. Even on main roads the pace is slow, with a maximum speed limit of 35mph (56kmh). Not that the sedate speed limits deter the island's affluent residents from driving around in their plush Porsches. Walking and cycling may be encouraged but Guernsey has one of the highest rates of private vehicle ownership in the world. If you are hiring a car be prepared for traffic congestion, very narrow lanes and a quaint but frustrating absence of signposting.

LOCATION AND CLIMATE

Guernsey lies in the Gulf of St Malo, 31 miles (50km) west of the Normandy coast and 75 miles (120km) south of Weymouth. As a bailiwick it also embraces the smaller islands of Herm, Jethou, Sark and Alderney. Herm and Sark can be easily reached by ferry (20 and 50 minutes respectively) while

Alderney post box and telephone kiosk

Alderney, the most northerly of the Channel Islands, just 8 miles (13km) from France, is more remote, taking 85 minutes by boat. In the summer the islands have a daily average of eight hours of sunshine and an average maximum temperature of 68°F (20°C). The best months to visit are from May to September, July and August being the hottest. Sea temperatures are chilly or refreshing, depending on how hardy you are, averaging 62.8°F (17.1°C) in summer.

'PECULIAR OF THE CROWN'

The Channel Islands have a quirky history and some unique, quasi-feudal customs. Termed a 'Peculiar of the Crown' they pledge allegiance directly to the English Crown, not to the parliament of the UK. As the last remaining territories of the dukes of Normandy, they toast the Queen of England as 'Our Duke of Normandy'. They are not full members of the EU, although when Britain joined (the then EEC) in 1973, they were granted special privileges. The islands delegate matters of foreign policy and defence to the UK parliament but in other affairs they guard their independence zealously. Guernsey has its own government and legal system; it prints its own currency (including a £1 note) and issues its own stamps. Sark's constitution dates back to

1563 and its feudal form of government prevailed up until 2008 when, after months of infighting, the island held its first general election and Sark became Europe's newest democracy.

LANGUAGE

Guernésiais (also known as patois, Dgernésiais and Guernsey French) is the local dialect, derived from ancient Norman French. It was once the island's native tongue but has now all but disappeared as a language spoken in the home.

Large numbers of English settlers arrived on Guernsey in the 19th century, many of them officers retired on half pay, and by the end of the century English was the prevalent language of St Peter Port. The use of the dialect as the island's first language came to an end in the post-war period when the many children who had been evacuated during the German Occupation returned to the island speaking English. In all the country parishes, however, Guernésiais could still be heard

⊙ FRENCH SPICE

On a clear day you can see the French coast from Guernsey's Jerbourg Point. Geographically the Channel Islands belong naturally to France rather than to England and have a discernible Gallic veneer. The great French Impressionist, Pierre-Auguste Renoir, who appraised Guernsey's light with a painter's eye at Moulin Huet Bay, noticed how 'the Anglo-Saxon miss sheds her prudery when she arrives in Guernsey'. Victor Hugo, for his part, was prepared to broaden her mind still further: ignoring Anglo-Saxon decencies altogether, he lived on the island with both wife and mistress, introducing them respectively as 'Madame, la mère de mes enfants' and 'Madame, mon amie'.

spoken until the late 1960s. The written language can still be seen today in street names and surnames, and the Guernsey Tourist Information Office welcomes you with *'Bian v'nue a tous'*. A small number of over 65s speak Guernésiais but as a visitor you are unlikely to hear it apart from the occasional greeting between locals. Sercquiais, Sark's equivalent to Guernésiais, has also virtually disappeared as a spoken language.

ECONOMY

Guernsey saw major changes during the late 20th century as the financial services industry took over from agriculture and tourism as the mainstay of the economy. The financial sector is now completely dominant, generating at least 40 percent of the island's economic output and employing nearly 20 percent of the island's workforce. Some of the traditional activities, such as dairy farming and fishing, still survive and recent years have seen the growth of small-scale producers including cheese-makers, organic farmers and specialist pig breeders.

The tourist industry started after World War II when curious sightseers arrived to see the relics of the German Occupation. From the 1950s it became a holiday paradise with a unique position close to France together with well-run, reasonably-priced hotels and guesthouses. Tourism reached its peak in the 1980s, then suffered a decline with competition from package holidays and low-cost carriers to the Mediterranean. A fortnight's holiday to the Channel Islands is now a thing of the past and the emphasis is on upmarket short breaks. In 2008, visitors to Guernsey increased following the publication of the novel *The Literary & Potato Peel Pie Society*, which is set on the island during the German Occupation. A film version of the book is due to be released in 2018, which is expected to boost tourism to the island further.

A BRIEF HISTORY

It was around 8500 BC that Guernsey became an island, cut off from the landmass of Europe by rising sea levels. Jersey was separated 2,000 years later. Given the vulnerable location of the Channel Islands it was inevitable that they became stepping stones for plundering armies on their way to new conquests. For centuries the islands were prey to scourges of nature, easy pickings for passing pirates and reluctant pawns passed between warring rulers. Reminders of the past are scattered around Guernsey, from prehistoric graves to anti-French fortifications and chilling war tunnels from the German Occupation.

EARLY HISTORY

At the august Royal Guernsey Golf Club, the archaeological equivalent of a hole in one was achieved in 1976 just alongside the fifth green: an array of protruding stones revealed under the gorse. Artefacts discovered at the dig date back to around 4500 BC and experts rate the site, called Les Fouaillages, as one of the oldest manmade structures ever found in Europe. Later evidence of the Neolithic culture on the islands are passage graves

Millenium Stone,
L'Ancresse Common

St Tugual Chapel

(tombs reached by tunnel), menhirs (tall monumental stones) and dolmens (stone slabs arranged as tombs). This is proof that the Neolithic residents of the Channel Islands, who lived here until around 2000 BC, had the technology to move 10-ton stones, as well as sufficient devotion to build imperishable monuments to their princes and gods.

During the Bronze and Iron ages, the Channel Islands had trade links with Britain, Ireland and France, and several sites have been discovered on Guernsey. In 1983 a rich Bronze Age site was excavated on the Hougue du Catelain at L'Ancresse, revealing large quantities of pottery, along with arrow heads, loom weights and other artefacts.

ROMANS AND CHRISTIANS

Opinion is divided whether or not the Romans colonised the islands, but they certainly passed through. In 1985 a 75ft (23-metre) -long Gallo-Roman vessel was discovered in St Peter's Port harbour. This flat-bottomed vessel, dating to around 180 AD and known to be the Roman ship 'Asterix', contained pottery, coins and a cargo of roof tiles. Castle Cornet's Maritime Museum devotes a section to the shipwreck and the preserved oak beams from the vessel will be on display in St Peter Port when a suitable site is found.

Christianity was established in the islands by the 6th century. The early Christian era was one of comparative peace, with parishes growing up around stone churches. But the peace was shattered in the 9th century when the Vikings arrived in their Scandinavian long ships, raiding the Normandy peninsula and Channel Islands. Over many years houses were burnt, islanders murdered, crops and cattle carried off and prehistoric tombs rifled. But the Norsemen were also expert sailors and farmers – skills which they left the islanders as a permanent legacy. They finally gained control of Normandy from Charles the Simple of France and in the 10th century the Duchy of Normandy expanded to the Channel Islands. The Normans made their mark here with their feudal laws, seafaring traditions and language.

THE BRITISH CONNECTION

Following the victory of Norman Duke William II (William the Conqueror) at the Battle of Hastings in 1066 the Channel

⊙ INSTANT JUSTICE

For more than a thousand years any Channel Islander has been able to get what amounts to an on-the-spot injunction to stop an alleged injustice against property. The wronged party invokes the Clameur de Haro, an ancient Norman cry for help said to have been created by Rollo the Viking who was made Duke of Normandy. If a civilian feels his property is being threatened he may go down on bended knee in the presence of two witnesses, and cry: 'Haro! Haro! Haro! A l'aide, mon prince, on me fait tort' ('O Rollo! O Rollo! To my aid, my prince, I am being wronged') followed by the Lord's Prayer in French. The accused then has to await the court's ruling on whether the Clameur has been correctly raised. To this day it survives as a fully enforceable law in Guernsey and Jersey, though it is rarely invoked.

Islands became part of the Anglo-Norman realm. This was the beginning of the link with the English Crown, reinforced in 1204 when King John lost Normandy to France. The Channel Islands were given the choice of remaining loyal to the English Crown or reverting to France. They opted for the former, and in return the king granted them 'the continuance of their ancient laws and privileges', laying the foundation for self-government. But England's hold over the islands transformed their nearest neighbour, France, into a perennial threat. Fear of invasion led to the construction of coastal fortifications and in 1204 Castle Cornet was built to command the east coast. Life under siege became so cruel that in 1483 Pope Sixtus IV issued a papal bull proclaiming the Channel Islands neutral.

At the outset of England's Civil War the town of St Peter Port and the castle that was intended to protect it were on opposite sides of the conflict. St Peter Port sided with the Parliamentarians whilst the governor of Guernsey supported the Royalist cause and holed up in Castle Cornet with his supporters. Besieged for no less than eight years, they fired some 30,000 cannon balls into Cromwell's St Peter Port.

NAVIGATION AND KNITTING

In the second half of the 17th century peace brought prosperity, which spread from the local grandees to merchants, sailors, and incipient industrialists. Privateering, whereby Channel Islands ships were licensed to capture enemy vessels and confiscate their cargoes, became a major source of revenue. As England imposed duty on imported luxury goods to fund its wars with France, Spain and the American colonies, Guernsey became a major supplier in the smuggling trade, shipping large quantities of captured bread, perfume and lace to England. This legalised piracy led to the development of a sizeable shipbuilding industry.

Meanwhile trade in wool between Southampton and the Channel Islands led to the rapid growth of the knitwear industry with the islands exporting high-quality sweaters, stockings and gloves to England and France. Knitting in fact became so popular and lucrative, with fishermen and farmers taking it up as well as women and children, that the harvest crops and seaweed collection began to suffer. A moratorium on knitting was imposed forbidding the making of stockings during harvest and vraicing (seaweed collection).

Jersey's privateering activities in the 1770s led to two attempts by France to capture the island, first in 1779 and more famously in the Battle of Jersey in 1781 when the heroic Major Francis Peirson led the local militia to victory. This was the last attempt by France to capture either island. But the fear of further invasions led both Jersey and Guernsey to construct dozens of Martello towers around the coasts, many of which can be seen today.

THE VICTORIAN ERA

A period of prosperity followed the English victories at Trafalgar in 1805 and Waterloo in 1815. Retired army and navy officers began to settle on the islands, attracted by the low cost of living. But even though hostilities officially ceased after the defeat of Napoleon there was still

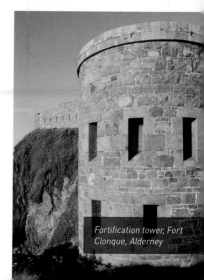

Fortification tower, Fort Clonque, Alderney

suspicion between England and France, a legacy of which are the Victorian defensive fortifications and notably Alderney's Braye Breakwater (1847–64). The intention was to convert Braye harbour into a massive naval base with a breakwater at each side of the bay. Only the western wall was built, originally a mile (1.5km) long.

Ship-owning in Jersey and Guernsey expanded rapidly in the first half of the 19th century, ranking the islands 10th among British ports in 1865, ahead even of Hull and Bristol. The growth was powered initially by oyster fishing and the cod trade, but gradually international shipping became more important, with Channel Island vessels, many of them built locally, travelling as far as Australia. But when iron steamships began to dominate the seas in the 1870s the islands were badly hit: the local ship build-ers couldn't afford to build them and local ship owners couldn't afford to buy them. The great seafaring days were over and the islanders turned to agriculture and tourism.

THE GERMAN OCCUPATION

The Channel Islands were the only British territory to fall into German hands dur-ing World War II. Tiny they may have been but Hitler saw them as the first step to his intended invasion of the United Kingdom. In 1940 Churchill decided that the islands, which had no strategic value for Britain, could not justify the cost of

---

Life in a Small World

If you read just one book on Guernsey make it *The Book of Ebenezer Le Page* by G.B. Edwards, the highly entertaining and mov-ing reminiscences of an 80-year-old recluse on his life on Guernsey in the 20th century and his despair at the trappings of modern-ism. It was the only novel by Guernsey-born G.B. Edwards, but has received much critical acclaim since its posthumous publication.

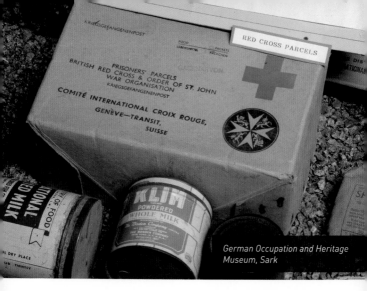

German Occupation and Heritage Museum, Sark

defence and the decision was taken that they should be demilitarised. This was to be part of Hitler's Atlantic Wall project, a line of defence works extending all the way from the Baltic to the Spanish frontier.

Prior to the arrival of Hitler's troops thousands of islanders, including almost the entire population of Alderney, fled to England, fearing the worst. The islands were turned into impregnable fortresses, with thousands of foreign forced labourers and Russian prisoners-of-war toiling in harsh conditions to construct concrete walls, command posts, bunkers and gun emplacements around the islands. Hitler believed that the Allies would eventually seek to retake the Channel islands and forced labourers were put to work on the German military hospital (see page 43), built underground to cater for hundreds of German casualties in the event of an attack. The allied landings never happened, the space was used to store munitions stock-piled by the Germans, the medical equipment was removed and today it is dimly lit, dank and cavernous – a sombre memorial to the slave workers who died here.

Following the D-Day landings the supply lines used by Germans through France were cut off and both civilians and occupying soldiers suffered hardship and deprivation. During the last months the near-starving population was saved by the Swedish SS *Vega*, bringing Red Cross food parcels and other essential provisions. On 9 May 1945 British forces liberated the Channel Islands and the occupying forces surrendered peacefully. Citizens gathered to listen to Churchill's broadcast of the German capitulation: 'And our dear Channel Islands are also to be freed today.' Liberation Day on 9 May has been celebrated ever since and especially so in 2015, the 70th anniversary of Liberation.

POST WAR

At the end of the war German prisoners were put to work dismantling forests of barbed wire and digging up thousands of mines. Fortunately, the German Army had posted *Achtung!* warnings on the edge of minefields. After World War II the islands saw a boost in tourism from visitors curious to see the aftermath of the Occupation. Greenhouse horticulture thrived, peaking in the 1970s when nine million trays of tomatoes were being exported annually. Competition for the UK market however, particularly from the Dutch and Spanish, led to a dramatic decline in the industry. Since the 1980s finance has been the mainstay of the economy. Stable government and advantageous tax laws led to the development of international financial services. Tourism flourished up to the late 1980s but now accounts for less than 3 percent of GDP. Cruise ships calling in at St Peter Port have given the industry a bit of a boost in recent years, increasing the number of day visitors. The capital welcomes around 100 ships each year.

HISTORICAL LANDMARKS

c.8500 BC Guernsey cut off from mainland France by rising sea levels at the end of the last Ice Age.

4500 BC Construction of Les Fouaillages, Guernsey, the oldest of the passage graves.

AD 556 St Sampson brings Christianity to Guernsey.

933 Channel Islands annexed to the Duchy of Normandy.

1066 William the Conqueror, 10th Duke of Normandy, conquers England and establishes the first constitutional links between Britain and the Channel Islands.

1204 King John loses Normandy to France but the islands remain loyal to the English Crown and are granted self-government.

1250 Work on Castle Cornet begins.

1564 Helier de Carteret colonises Sark, setting up the feudal system.

1651 Castle Cornet is the last loyalist stronghold in the British Isles to surrender in the Civil War.

Mid-18th century Privateering (legal piracy) becomes a major source of revenue for the island.

1900 Guernsey's parliament adopts English as its official language.

1940 Channel Islands demilitarised and thousands are evacuated.

1940–4 The Germans occupy the islands, building substantial fortifications.

1945 German forces surrender unconditionally on 9 May.

1973 Britain joins the EEC (now the EU). Special terms are agreed for the Channel Islands.

2009 In Sark the new democratic Chief Pleas (legislative body) is sworn in after 450 years of feudalism.

2015 Celebrations on all the Channel Islands mark the 70th anniversary of Liberation from German occupying forces (9 May 1945).

2016 Vice Admiral Sir Ian Corder CB is sworn in as Lieutenant Governor of the Bailiwick of Guernsey, succeeding Air Marshal Peter Walker, who died in the post.

2018 Guernsey's government votes against assisted dying being made legal on the island.

St Peter Port harbour

WHERE TO GO

Guernsey is a tiny island of 24 sq miles (62 sq km) miles and it is only 10 miles (16km) by road between the two furthest points on the island. Bear in mind though that journeys, particularly in built-up areas, can be very time-consuming.

Guernsey is divided up into 10 parishes, not that you would be aware which one you were in when driving around. The island is roughly triangular in shape and divides into two quite distinct parts: to the south and east is the cliff-fringed 'high parish' region where access to the beach is via deep wooded valleys or steep rock-cut steps. The 'low parish' region to the north and west of the islands consists of flat land fringed by miles of sand dunes.

Many visitors choose to stay in or close to St Peter Port, justifiably described as one of Europe's most appealing harbour towns. It is the hub of the island with the best choice of restaurants, shops and sightseeing on the island. Beach lovers and extreme sports enthusiasts should head for the west coast, fringed by fine sandy beaches; keen walkers to the south coast for 28 miles (44.5km) of footpaths along the flower-clad cliffs. The peaceful little sister islands of Herm, Sark and Alderney offer the ultimate escape from the stresses of life.

ST PETER PORT

Hugging the slopes that rise steeply back from the sea, Guernsey's captivating capital, **St Peter Port ❶**, creates a spectacular vista as you arrive by sea. Church

Tourist Information

A good place to begin exploring the town is the excellent Guernsey Information Centre (www.visitguernsey.com) on North Esplanade, with its informative displays and helpful staff.

spires and steep-roofed granite houses are stacked on the hill-side while in the harbour below the forest of boat masts jostle for attention, lending the capital an almost Mediterranean air.

The discovery of a Roman wreck in the harbour in 1985 indicated that this part of Guernsey's coastline was a refuge for seamen even in ancient times. The Town Church existed as early as 1048 and a castle has stood here since 1206, though today's town is made up mainly of finely preserved late Georgian and Regency buildings.

In former times fishing was the main activity, and St Peter Port was merely a small quayside settlement. It was through privateering or licensed piracy (see page 18) that the town grew in size and wealth. Wealthy merchants built fine houses and new buildings spread up the slopes around the town and onto the plateau above. Today 'Town', as the islanders call it, is a charming centre of narrow cobbled shopping streets and thoroughfares, with tantalising glimpses of the harbour and castle.

THE WATERFRONT

The whole harbour front has been reclaimed from the sea. Originally ships would have docked right alongside the warehouses that line **Quayside** (now converted to restaurants and shops) enabling cargoes of wine, citrus fruits, spices, sugar and wool to be lifted straight from the ship's hold into the tall Dutch-style warehouses. Linking Quayside and the High Street are a number of steep lanes, called *venelles* (Guernsey-French dialect for 'little passages'). Look up as you explore them – some are roofed over using massive timbers from broken-up ships. Between Victoria (or Crown) Pier and Albert Pier lies the old harbour where yachts, fishing craft, dinghies and inter-island ferries busily cross paths and the halyards of moored yachts clink as their crews sun themselves on deck.

The less picturesque St Julian's Pier to the north was added in the 1920s to make way for cargo ships and ferries. Today high-speed catamarans sail for mainland Britain and France. At the landward end, the Travel Trident kiosk sells tickets for ferries to Herm, the diminutive car-free island which you can see in the distance. Further along the pier you can purchase ferry tickets for Sark, another popular day trip island, one step further to the southeast.

Along the Waterfront

At the landward end of St Julian's Pier is the **Liberation Monument** Ⓐ, a granite 'needle' erected in 1995 to commemorate the 50th anniversary of the island's liberation from occupying German forces on 9 May 1945. It was here that crowds of islanders greeted the British liberators after five years under German rule. On Liberation Day each year, and only on this

Discovery Pass

A Discovery Pass, available from the Guernsey Information Centre or at the museums, allows unlimited entry to Castle Cornet, the Guernsey Museum at Candie and Fort Grey, with accompanying children going free.

day, the monument casts a shadow onto the plaques on the adjacent granite bench, each marking a key event of that jubilant day. The monument is designed so that the tip of the shadow reaches each plaque at the precise time of the event it commemorates. On 9 May 2015, the 70th anniversary of Liberation, Guernsey residents and visitors celebrated with a Calvacade, re-enactments and a host of entertainment and activities. Celebratory events throughout the Channel Islands stretched over five weeks in April and May.

A prominent landmark on The Quay is the majestic **Town Church B** whose sturdy steeple you can see rising above the waterfront as you arrive by sea. Although the building incorporates the nave of the medieval church, much of the original fabric was damaged during the Civil War and it underwent major restoration in the 19th century. The church has served many civic purposes through the years including the storage of fire engines and guns. The stained-glass windows replace those shattered in 1944 by an American bomb intended for a suspected German submarine in the harbour.

CASTLE CORNET

Built to protect the settlement in the 13th century, **Castle Cornet C** (www.museums.gov.gg; daily, mid-Feb–late Mar 10am–3pm, late Mar–early Nov 10am–5pm, July–Aug from 9.30am, guided tours most days at 10.30am) was formerly isolated on a rocky islet, and accessible only by boat. Today you can reach it along Castle Pier (the most southerly of the piers). A great breakwater stretches beyond the castle, with a light-house at the far end where anglers cast their lines. A third of the way along the pier you can divert left to **Fish Quay**, where the workaday fishing boats land their catch and gulls swoop down in the hope of tasty morsels.

Enjoying fine views of neighbouring Havelet Bay and the town skyline, the castle is a delightful maze of buildings and courtyards, linked by steps and passageways, and enhanced by carefully nurtured gardens. The castle was a stronghold of the English Crown for nearly 800 years, built when King John lost Normandy to the French in 1204, then developed and expanded over the centuries. It has been a low-profile fort since 1672, when lightning touched off the ammunition stores, bringing down the

Castle Cornet at night

towering central keep and killing the governor's wife and mother, and five other people. But much of the medieval military architecture is remarkably complete. The superb views from the citadel explain the presence of German gun emplacements there. The Germans occupied the castle during World War II and had to make very few modifications to fit it for modern warfare.

The monument is surprisingly big – allow plenty of time if you want to see all the specialist museums and try to time your visit to coincide with the **noon-day gun ceremony**, when two redcoats fire an artillery salute to St Peter Port. Beware the sudden roar! **The Story of Castle Cornet** in the Lower Barracks (opposite the ticket office) traces the turbulent history of the castle using a series of reconstructions, replicas, models and original artefacts. Objects displayed include the Guernsey Falcon, an artillery piece cast in 1550. There are Guernsey-themed military and RAF museums, and an absorbing **Maritime Museum** in the Upper Barracks. This starts with prehistoric trade when stone axes were bartered for grain and fish, and ends with the modern era of high-speed catamarans. One section is devoted to Asterix, a Gallo-Roman wreck which came to grief in AD 286 in the mouth of the harbour, with a video telling of its

Le Vallette Underground Military Museum

discovery and salvage in 1982. Maritime exhibits include colourful ships' figureheads, privateer licences and Victor Hugo's personal lifebelt and lifejacket – the writer was deeply interested in the question of safety at sea and commissioned his own special safety equipment.

From Easter to the end of September, the Guernsey History in Action Company (www.ghiac.org) re-enacts stories from Guernsey's past from Neolithic times to World War II. Performances take place daily in the castle grounds, and usually last 15–20 minutes. Look out too for outdoor theatre performances in the castle grounds in summer and other events.

LA VALETTE UNDERGROUND MILITARY MUSEUM

Just to the south, along the coastal road, is a tunnel complex built by slave labourers during the German Occupation, now occupied by **La Valette Underground Military Museum** Ⓓ (www.lavalette.tk; Mar–mid-Nov daily 10am–5pm). The tunnels served as a refuelling station for U-boats, and one of the huge fuel oil storage tanks can still be seen. The museum is packed with World War I and II military and civilian memorabilia. Along with many uniforms and medals, there are World War II posters detailing the evacuation of the islands in 1940, notices to shoot locals committing larceny and a display of Red Cross food parcels delivered by the Swedish ship, the SS *Vega*, towards the end of the war when the population of the Channel Islands was close to starving. Whips and rubber truncheons bring home the brutal nature of the treatment of the slave labourers who built the tunnels.

Across the road from the museum the seafront promenade affords fine views of Castle Cornet and neighbouring islands. At low tide you can spot **La Vallette Bathing Pools**, public swimming pools since Victorian times. The first was the Horseshoe, built in 1859 with a small dressing room, then the Ladies and Gents in 1876 and the Children's pool added in 1896. Today all four pools – when they are not submerged by the tides – are open to all, free of charge.

THE AQUARIUM

The South Esplanade continues a short way to another tunnel: this one was built in 1861, as part of a scheme, never completed, for building a road through to Fermain Bay (see page 40). The Germans constructed several side tunnels, using Russian labourers who left their hammer and sickle symbol on the rocky roof.

Today the tunnels house **The Aquarium** Ⓔ (tel: 01481-723 301; daily 9am–5pm, shorter hours in winter), displaying examples of the many and varied fish to be found in Guernsey's waters – from perfectly camouflaged baby soles and the tiny inhabitants of tidal pools to larger conger eels and dogfish. There are also prettily patterned tropical fish, with notes on their habitats and suitability for use in home aquariums, a collection of reptiles in a vivarium and a terrapin island. Fish are fed two or three times a week on squid, beef heart, sand eel and sprats; lizards are treated with fresh fruit and live insects such as crickets and locusts.

THE HEART OF TOWN

Behind the Town Church **Market Square** Ⓕ underwent a multimillion-pound restoration and the 19th-century market is now a 21st-century shopping mall of high street names and local traders. Produce from across the island is brought to the weekly Fresh Friday market, while on Saturdays in summer the square is the venue for open-air concerts and drama.

Even if you aren't a keen shopper, it's worth exploring the maze of the Arcades to the left as you emerge from Market Street, along with the cobbled **High Street** and its extension, **Le Pollet**. The best known thoroughfares of St Peter Port, these appealing streets are always busy by day. Many of the shops along here have tall and elegant Regency, Victorian and Edwardian facades.

At the junction of High Street and Le Pollet, Smith Street leads left and uphill towards the **Royal Court House**, the former centre of island government and administration. The streets north of here (around Hospital Lane) are home to the hidden world of finance; only the gleaming brass plaques of fiducaries and trust corporations hint at the wheelings and dealings going on inside.

Candie Gardens

Greenhouse and ornamental gardens, Candie Gardens

CANDIE GARDENS AND GUERNSEY MUSEUM

Above the financial district the **Candie Gardens** Ⓖ (year-round until dusk; free) are late 19th-century pleasure gardens with wonderful views over the port and neighbouring islands. Brass bands strike up on summer Sunday afternoons at the Victorian bandstand where there is also an excellent café. Once part of a private estate, the gardens were bequeathed to the islanders in 1871 and turned into a public park. At the top stands a statue of Queen Victoria in imperial regalia with orb and sceptre. This is diplomatically separated from a more flamboyant statue of her critic, Victor Hugo, which was given to Guernsey by the French Government in thanks for the hospitality shown by the island to Hugo during his exile.

The bandstand is incorporated into the **Guernsey Museum at Candie** Ⓗ (www.museums.gov.gg; Apr–Oct 10am–5pm, Nov–Mar 10am–4pm), devoted to the island's archaeology, history and wildlife. Exhibits in the adjacent art gallery include Rodin's bust of Victor Hugo (1883), wearing a most expressive frown and wild beard and characterful sketches by Peter de Lièvre (1812–78) of island farmers and fishermen, giving an insight into life on the island in Victorian times. The gallery's permanent collection is put away when temporary exhibitions are on show.

GUERNSEY TAPESTRY

To the south on College Street is **St James**, a deconsecrated garrison church providing Guernsey with a versatile venue for concerts, drama, lectures and exhibitions. Part of the complex is the purposebuilt Dorey Centre, housing the **Guernsey Tapestry ❶** (www.guernseytapestry.org.gg; mid-Mar–Oct Mon–Sat 10am–4.30pm, Nov–Feb 11am–4pm). The display comprises 10 separate tapestries, each one representing a century of Guernsey's history. These accurate and meticulously worked scenes were created by the 10 Guernsey parishes to mark the new millennium and each one bears the crest of the relevant parish.

Opposite St James is the neo-Gothic bulk of Elizabeth College, founded as a school in the 16th century and rebuilt in the 1820s using the proceeds from a special tax of a shilling on every gallon of spirits sold on the island.

VICTORIAN SHOP AND PARLOUR

One of the best vantage points of St Peter Port is to be had from the top of Victor Hugo's house, one of Guernsey's star attractions. To reach the house walk up Cornet Street stopping en route at the **Victorian Shop and Parlour ❷** at 26 Cornet Street (Easter–Sept Tue–Sat 10am–4pm, limited opening during Dec for Christmas shopping; free). This well-preserved, quaint townhouse has a reconstituted parlour at the rear and a shop where volunteers in period costume sell traditional toys, souvenirs and sweets in glass jars which are measured in ounces and pounds. The building serves as the headquarters of the National Trust of Guernsey.

VICTOR HUGO'S HOUSE

From the Victorian shop you can climb up **Hauteville**, where the increasingly large and ornamented houses and villas give some indication of the status and wealth of the people who first settled here when the area began to be developed in the 1780s. The street's most famous resident was Victor Hugo, the great French romantic poet, writer and politician who lived for 15 years at No. 38, **Hauteville House** Ⓚ (tel: 01481-721 911; www.museums. gov.gg/hauteville; guided tours by appointment only, in English, French and German; closed for restoration until spring 2019).

Hugo was more than a little eccentric, and the house, owned by the city of Paris, is a physical manifestation of his quirky ideas about monarchy, history and patriarchy. Having been thrown out of France, branded as a dangerous radical for his opposition

⊙ FOREVER FRENCH

The French novelist, poet and political activist Victor Hugo (1802–85) was granted Guernsey citizenship, but he never learned to speak English. 'When England wants to chat with me', he used to say, 'let her learn my language'. Throughout his life his heart always belonged to France and he would tell fellow exiles 'The tear in our eyes is called France.' Hugo's exile was spent in Jersey for three years, then in Guernsey for 15. Guernsey welcomed him and he returned the affection. His book, *Les Travailleurs de la Mer* (*The Toilers of the Sea*) is dedicated to 'the rock of hospitality and freedom....the island of Guernsey, severe and gentle'.

Victorian Shop and Parlour

to the *coup d'état* staged by Prince Louis Napoleon in 1851, Hugo first settled in Jersey, where he kept up a tirade against *'Napoléon le petit'* as he styled the French emperor, through his newspaper, *L'Homme*. In the same paper, he criticised Queen Victoria for making a state visit to Paris in 1855. This so angered the people of Jersey that Hugo was expelled once again – this time moving a short distance north to the island of Guernsey. Here he installed his wife (*'Madame, la mère de mes enfants'*) and family at Hauteville House, and Juliette Drouet, his mistress (*'Madame, mon amie'*) at No. 20 Hauteville, which had been his first Guernsey home. This was sufficiently close for Hugo to signal to his mistress from his bedroom window.

Whilst living here Hugo wrote some of his best-selling novels, including *Les Misérables* and *Les Travailleurs de la Mer (The Toilers of the Sea)* which is set in and around Guernsey and demonstrates Hugo's intimate knowledge of the island. Growing wealthy for the first time, Hugo indulged his taste for wood-working and interior decoration. He bought chests and pews and broke them up to line the walls and ceilings of his rooms, adding his own embellishments and VH initials to create a house that is dark, brooding, lavishly decorated and full of symbolic meaning. Significantly, he chose to write his powerfully romantic novels in a room that was, by contrast with the rest of the house, flooded with light – he constructed a rooftop observatory of glass, with far-reaching views over the blue seas to his beloved France.

You can view the building on a conducted tour, though the eminently knowledgeable guides make this one of the best places you can visit anywhere on the Channel Islands.

In the garden, now restored, Hugo planted an acorn for a tree which, ahead of his era, he christened 'the oak of the United States of Europe'.

SOUTHERN GUERNSEY

The south coast, where steep granite cliffs tower above secluded little bays, couldn't be more of a contrast to the flat beaches of the west. Footpaths run all the way along the cliffs, dipping down to tiny coves where the retreating tide reveals sandy beaches, some only accessible by foot. The walk along here is the most exhilarating and spectacular of the island. There is plenty for sightseers too, with a fine old manor house and gardens, German Occupation museums and 'the smallest chapel in the world'.

SAUSMAREZ MANOR

South of St Peter Port, off the Sausmarez Road, lies the strong-hold of one of Guernsey's oldest families: **Sausmarez Manor 2** (www.sausmarezmanor.co.uk; grounds daily 10am–5pm, free apart from Subtropical Gardens and Art Park; house tours

June–Sept Mon–Thu 10.30am, 11.30am and 2.30pm, first half Apr and second half of Oct Mon–Thu 11.30am, mid-Apr–May and first half of Oct Mon–Thu 10.30am and 11.30am). The de Sausmarez family have lived here since 1254, and a fine series of family portraits hangs in the imposing grey granite house, which dates from 1714. The family has been one of Guernsey's most distinguished dynasties, having served as bailiffs, governors, naval officers and diplomats. The manor is still lived in and you may well come across the Seigneur, Peter de Sausmarez, chatting to visitors. He also takes the evening Ghost Tours.

Manor Gardens

Surrounding the house are delightfully informal gardens, where you might possibly trip over free-range ducks and hens

Moulin Huet Bay

Sausmarez Manor Farmers' Market

scrabbling for food in the undergrowth. Attractions include a **pitch-and-putt course**, a **Coppersmiths' Workshop** in the Tudor Barn where the craftsman is the only surviving coppersmith to make the traditional Guernsey milk cans in the time-honoured way, a **ride-on 7¼-gauge trains** and children's play area, a craft shop and a tearoom in the old vinery by the lakeside, and a gallery with gifts and home furnishings. Don't miss the **Artparks**, one of the largest and most varied sculpture parks in Britain, set amid subtropical woodland. Showing around 220 works by 90 artists, this is a fascinating collection, from life-size figures to flying frogs, with a surprise around every corner.

If you happen to be here on a Saturday you're in for a treat. The **Farmers' Market** is held in the grounds from 9am–12.45pm and has a wonderful range of local produce: chancre and spider crabs, local beef and pork, free-range eggs, cheeses, Guernsey *gâche* (fruit loaf) and home-made cakes and pies. You will also find handmade arts and crafts, bric-à-brac, jewellery, antiques and plants.

FERMAIN BAY

East of Sausmarez Manor lies one of Guernsey's prettiest beaches, **Fermain Bay** ❸. Bobbing with boats and washed by gentle waves, the bay has the air of the Mediterranean. This is a lovely spot for sunbathing, swimming in the sparkling waters (though sand is only exposed at low tide) and diving from the steps. Despite being one of Guernsey's most picturesque spots, the bay is rarely crowded since the only vehicular access is by a private road, closed to all but permit holders, and there is no nearby parking. This does not put off the punters coming by day or evening to the Fermain Beach Café, one of Guernsey's top café/restaurants and an ideal spot for a break.

JERBOURG POINT

On the southeast corner of the island **Jerbourg Point** ❹ has the most compelling views on the south coast. With good visibility you can see Jersey to the south, the other Channel Islands to the east, and the coast of Normandy beyond. From the most southerly tip of the point you can see six rock formations known as the Pea Stacks of the East or **Les Tas de Pois d'Amont**. The rocks look like monks (especially from a boat), with stooped backs and deep pointed hoods – particularly the middle stack, which is known as Le Petit Bonhomme d'Andriou (The Little Good Man Andrew). The story goes that Andriou, a pagan priest, witnessed a ship heading for the rocks in a storm and prayed to his gods to calm the waves. The weather only worsened so he then beseeched the Christian God, vowing to become a Christian if his prayers were answered. The ship was saved, Andriou was baptised and built a chapel on the site. In bygone days sailors used to pay their respects as they sailed past Andriou. Today the stacks are a habitat for nesting birds.

The cliff path which you can pick up on the Jerbourg peninsula goes all the way west to Pleinmont (see page 48).

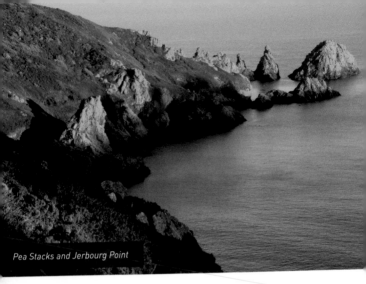

Pea Stacks and Jerbourg Point

MOULIN HUET BAY

A steep path near Doyle's Monument leads down to **Petit Port ⑤**. This is one of Guernsey's loveliest beaches and when the tide rolls out to reveal the sandy expanse, it's a perfect spot for bathing, provided you don't mind the return climb up 270 steps! The cliff path westwards from Petit Port leads to the gorgeous **Moulin Huet Bay ⑥**. If going by car, follow the signs from the main road after Sausmarez Manor, then it's a 5-minute walk down a steep path. With its striking rock formations, caves and waterfall, the bay is best enjoyed when the water is at half-tide or below, as the loveliest bits are covered by water at high tide. The French Impressionist painter, Pierre-Auguste Renoir, was so captivated by the bay's rock pools, cliffs and sea caves he painted no fewer than 15 pictures of the scenic cove on a painting trip to Guernsey in 1883.

LA GRAN'MÈRE DE CHIMQUIÈRE

Guernsey's most appealing piece of prehistory stands in the most unlikely spot for a pagan monument: at the entrance to the graveyard of St Martin's Church. This is in the village of St Martin a short way inland from the coast. The **Gran'mère de Chimquière** ❼ (Grandmother of the Cemetery) is considerably older than most grandmothers and though stony faced she nevertheless flaunts her naked breasts. She was carved in the early Bronze Age, possibly 4,000 years ago and modified to represent a Mother Goddess about 2,000 years later. If you visit after a wedding Gran'mère is quite likely to be wearing a garland of flowers: newlyweds traditionally place flowers on her head for luck. The crack through the torso is believed to have been the result of an attack by a church warden who was angry over the worshipping of stone idols.

GERMAN UNDERGROUND MILITARY HOSPITAL

From St Martin's take the main road going west, signed to the airport, and in just over half a mile (0.8km) turn right following signs for the **German Underground Military Hospital** ❽ (Mon, Wed–Sun 10am–4pm, reduced opening hours in winter).

Tucked away down a green lane, this is one of the largest complexes in the

Gran'mère de Chimquière

German Underground Military Hospital

Channel Islands constructed during the Occupation era. The hospital is a testimony to Hitler's mistaken belief that the Allies would, as a matter of pride, eventually seek to attack and retake the Channel Islands. Hitler entrusted the task of fortifying the islands to Dr Fritz Todt, who had earlier been responsible for planning and building Germany's *autobahn* system. Organisation Todt, as it was known, involved turning the Channel Islands into an impregnable fortress, with artillery able to cover a whole sweep of the French coast.

This hospital, along with its counterpart in Jersey, was intended for the treatment of hundreds of German military casualties in the event of an attack. Built underground, the wards and operating theatres were hewn out of solid rock by slave workers from Russia, Poland, Alsace and the Czech Republic, many of whom died as a result of the brutal treatment meted out by the German occupying forces.

The tunnels took more than three and a half years to build but were operational for only nine months. The expected Allied invasion never came and the occupying forces surrendered on 9 May 1945. Instead, the space was used principally to store the vast quantities of munitions stock-piled by the Germans.

Nearly all the military medical equipment was removed and as a result the Hospital is sombre and cavernous. Unlike its counterpart in Jersey there are only a handful of displays, and the dim lighting, damp concrete floors and the very emptiness of the place render it a chilling reminder of Guernsey under the jackboot.

THE LITTLE CHAPEL

Just west of this dank and chilly spot lies the **Little Chapel** ❾ (www.thelittlechapel.gg; open daily; free, donations encouraged) which is both kitsch and enchanting. The building is a complete church in miniature, and claims to be the smallest in the world. The chapel is modelled on the grotto in the Church of Lourdes and every square inch is encrusted with seashells, coloured pebbles and china and glass fragments. Barely 16ft (5 metres) in length, the chapel has difficulty accommodating even a dozen people. It is the third in a series of mini-chapels built on the site by a monk, Brother Deodat, in 1923–39 (a fellow monk added final touches in the years to 1965).

PETIT BÔT BAY

Back on the south coast some of the island's most attractive 'water lanes' (or lush valleys) run down to **Petit Bôt Bay** ❿. This attractive cove is a popular bathing spot, and one of the island's sunniest and most sheltered

The Little Chapel

Martyn Guille

Close to the Little Chapel you'll find the Martyn Guille Gold and Silver Workshop (www.martynguille.com; daily 9am–5pm, closed Sun in winter; free), where you can watch craftsmen at work and browse the showroom. Among the items made here are the famous Guernsey milk cans. A large range of clocks is also on display.

bays. Arrive early as parking space is limited. A Napoleonic-era loophole tower stands guard over the bay, and what was once an old mill is now occupied by a café with a sea view. The brooks that run down the sides of the green lanes used to power two mills, one of which was used for paper-making.

GERMAN OCCUPATION MUSEUM

German bunkers and artillery lookouts are the most tangible testament to wartime days, but they convey little of life at the time. The **German Occupation Museum** ⓫ (www.german occupationmuseum.co.uk; daily, Apr–Oct 10am–4.30pm, Nov–Mar 10am–1pm), behind Forest Church and signed off the main road, fills the gap. This is an absorbing war museum founded in 1966 by Richard Hearne who was a child during the German Occupation and still oversees the museum.

Among the many exhibits is a large painting depicting a Rhine Valley scene, complete with castle and vineyards, painted on the walls of a nearby house by a homesick soldier. Another rarity is a stone painted with a red V (for Victory) sign. Guernsey people showed their defiance by painting such signs wherever they could until the occupying troops took to painting laurel wreaths underneath to represent German victory. There are informers' letters, a horse's gas mask, some wartime condoms (German issue), a doll's house made from cardboard boxes and letters from the Controlling Committee of the States of Guernsey giving instructions for the distribution of food during the dark days towards the end of the war when food was desperately short. Surprisingly, cigarettes did not need to be rationed – experiments in growing tobacco on Guernsey proved very successful, ensuring an unlimited supply of locally made cigarettes. The reconstruction of a wartime kitchen on Guernsey, with recipes for marrow pudding and potato sponge, tell of civilian hardships. Street scenes from St Peter Port show hungry locals queueing outside the butcher's for a ration of meat in 1941.

PLEINMONT HEADLAND

The main road to the Pleinmont Headland goes takes you past **Torteval Church** with a distinctive round tower and witch's-hat

Petit Bôt Bay

spire. Standing prominently on the windy headland to the west is the **Pleinmont Observation Tower** ⑫ (Apr–Oct Sun and Wed 2–4.30pm, last entry 4pm), a fully-restored World War II naval observation tower, pierced by viewing slots. It was from here that German observers controlled Guernsey's coastal artillery, communicating with the gunners by radio.

On the same headland to the north is the **Table des Pions**, also known as 'The Fairy Ring', a grassy mound encircled by a ditch. This spot played a prominent role in a medieval ceremony, the *Chevauchée de St Michel*, when officers of the feudal court inspected the highways and sea defences to ensure that local landowners were fulfilling their duty to maintain them. The pions were the footmen who accompanied the officers and the Table des Pions was the spot where they took a break to enjoy an open-air banquet.

⊘ SOUTH COAST CLIFF PATH

The footpath along the south coast cliffs is the most spectacular and challenging walk on the island. It is 15 miles (24km) from St Peter Port all the way to Pleinmont Headland in the west. The walk can either be done in its entirety over a long day, or in separate shorter sections at a gentler pace. The path requires some stamina, especially for the steep climbs up and down from the bays, but you can take breaks at beachside cafés. The walk can be done at any time of year, but the scenery is at its best in spring when wild flowers carpet the cliffs and birds come ashore to nest. Don't forget to bring binoculars to spot fulmars, cormorants, shags, and the gannets and puffins that nest on offshore islets. Dolphins, grey seals and basking sharks are also occasionally spotted from the cliff paths.

THE WEST COAST

Wide sandy beaches, where islanders come to play, are the big attractions of the west coast. Vazon Bay is a magnet for the island's extreme sports enthusiasts, luring surfers when the conditions are right, while Cobo Bay is the most popular beach for families. For diversions from the beaches there are burial chambers, coastal forts, Lihou Island (when the tide is right) and, inland, Saumarez Park.

Fort Grey at dusk

ROCQUAINE BAY

Merging with L'Erée Bay, **Rocquaine Bay** ⑬ is over 1 mile (1.6km) long with alternating beaches and rocky outcrops. At low tide it forms one continuous stretch of sand – Guernsey's biggest beach, with safe swimming and rock pools to explore. During late July to early August the beach is the main focus of the Rocquaine Regatta, a full day and evening of free entertainment and whacky events like raft racing. To the south lies **Portelet,** a quiet sandy cove at the foot of the south coast cliffs that boasts a small working harbour. If the tide is out, Portelet is a brilliant place for a swim. Alternatively, there is a prettily-sited tea garden at the top with sweeping views.

Le Creux ès Faies dolmen

FORT GREY

At the southern end of the bay, **Fort Grey** ⑭ was built in 1804 as part of Sir John Doyle's grand scheme for defending Guernsey against potential attack from Napoleon's army. With its outer curtain wall and inner tower, the fort is affectionately known as the Cup and Saucer. The excellent **Shipwreck Museum** (www.museums.gov.gg; late Mar–Oct daily 10am–4.30pm) is housed within the tower and could not be in a more appropriate setting: overlooking the graveyard of more than 90 recorded shipwrecks.

The treacherous rock-strewn coasts and strong currents around the Channel Islands have always posed a hazard for ships. From the earliest seafaring days two crucial trade routes passed close to Guernsey: from Britain and northern Europe to the Mediterranean and from the English Channel to America. But it was the 19th-century surge in trade that led to the largest number of disasters. In bad weather captains would mistake the Channel Islands for the south coast of England and steer south, intending to head into the middle of the Channel, but unfortunately aiming straight at the reefs. One of the worst disastersthe railway steamer, SS *Stella*, which ran into fog and struck the Casquets in 1898. The boat sank within eight minutes of impact, and 105 people lost their lives. Building a lighthouse on the Hanois reef in 1862 reduced the annual toll of shipwrecks, and in 1975 the shipping lane for ocean-going vessels was moved 10 miles (16km) west to avoid further casualties.

The Shipwreck Museum tells the grim story of many of the local shipwrecks and displays salvaged treasures, from a ship's bell and a fine candelabra to coffee pots from the SS *Yorouba*, which foundered in 1888.

⊙ A GUERNSEY TO WEAR

Channel Islanders have been busy knitting since the 15th century. Queen Elizabeth was in favour of Guernsey stockings and Mary Queen of Scots even wore a pair to her own execution. Knitting became so lucrative that fishermen and farmers took it up as well as women and children. While the word 'jersey' has entered the English language, the stylish Guernsey is far less well known. It was originally made for seamen, the tightly knitted stitches producing a hard-wearing garment. By the 19th century the Guernsey had become well known and Nelson adopted it as standard issue for the English navy. Today one of the few outlets where you can find Guernseys is Le Tricoteur, next to Guernsey Pearl on Rocquaine Bay. If you are wondering where the sheep are, most of the wool is imported.

L'ERÉE HEADLAND

To explore the headland at the northern tip of **L'Erée Bay** take the small road left off the main coast road (after the Taste of India restaurant) which leads to the headland. Just after the German bunker there is a small sign on the right to **Le Creux ès Faies** ⑮. This is the island's third largest megalithic tomb, a dolmen which you can crawl inside. The name means 'Cave of the Fairies' as it was believed that fairies came out on moonlit nights to dance on the nearby Catioroc headland. The prehistoric passage grave was probably built around 3000 BC and used for 1,000 years or more, with bodies and ashes being placed in the chambers, along with gifts of pottery, flint and stone tools.

Beyond the dolmen stands **Fort Saumarez** ⑯, a strange feat of World War II improvisation: a four-floor observation tower tacked on to an 18th-century Martello-style tower. The fort is named after Lord James Saumarez, who in 1794 defeated five attacking French frigates with his ship, HMS *Crescent*. The headland commands fine views of sweeping Rocquaine Bay to the south and Les Grandes Rocques to the north. A monument here commemorates those who lost their lives when MV *Prosperity* foundered on the reefs off Perelle Bay in January 1974 with the loss of all 16 crew.

LIHOU ISLAND

From the car park, a path leads down to the centuries-old causeway, which at low tide links mainland Guernsey to **Lihou Island** ⑰. This lovely windswept islet, the most westerly point of the Channel Islands, is now a nature reserve, noted for its migrant seabirds, rabbits, resident peacocks, sea clover and sea pinks. A notice at either end of the causeway gives the times when it may safely be crossed (the tide returns swiftly, and can cut you off). You can also find the times of the tides in *The Guernsey Press*, at Fort Grey or at www.gov.gg/article/120220/Tide-tables-and-Lihou-causeway.

Apart from its walks and wildlife, Lihou is mainly of interest for the remains of the 12th-century Priory of St Mary, built by Benedictine monks who arrived from the Abbey of Mont St Michel in around 1114. Three dolmens and seven menhirs discovered by the monks were used as foundations for the chapel. The priory is believed to have been used until the 16th century, after which it became a farmhouse. During World War II the church was used as target practice by the Germans. Little now remains of the building, except a few wall fragments. Until 1994, when the States of Guernsey bought the island, a Guernsey law forbade all but islanders to make the crossing to Lihou.

View across to Lihou Island

Guernsey Pearl

If you visit the Guernsey Pearl jewellery shop (opposite Fort Grey) you won't find Guernsey pearls. They come from the Far East but are made up here. Visitors can watch the art of pearl stringing and purchase jewellery.

Beyond the priory, on the northwest coast, you can climb over rocks to the **Venus Pool**, large and deep enough to bathe in, but take heed of the signs discouraging access during the nesting season.

PERELLE BAY

The main road skirts the coast via L'Erée Shingle Bank towards **Perelle Bay**. At Le Catioroc, beside the Napoleonic Chinchon battery, **Le Trépied** is a prehistoric passage grave, reputed to be the place where local witches met with the devil for Friday-night revelries. Perelle Bay derives its name from the Celtic word for rock and at low tide you can see why. This used to be a favourite bay for collecting ormers, the indigenous mollusc prized for its mother-of-pearl inner shell as well as its flavour (see page 98).

ST APOLLINE'S CHAPEL

In the village of Perelle, **St Apolline's Chapel** ⓱ (open daylight hours; free), built in 1394, is a little medieval jewel, just by the roadside. It is the only chapel in the British Isles dedicated to Apolline, a deaconess martyred in 249 AD, who is regarded as the patron saint of dentistry. Fragments of frescoes depict the *Last Supper* and what is thought to be Christ washing the feet of Apostles. The chapel had been used as a cowshed before the States of Guernsey bought it in 1873 and rescued it from this humble role.

VAZON BAY

The biggest beach on the island, **Vazon Bay** 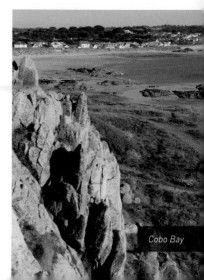 is the sports playground of the island, where Guernsey beach boys ride the rollers and shore fishermen bring in bass and mullet. To join the fun head for the Guernsey Surf School (www.guernseysurf-school.co.uk; tel: 07911-710 789) which offers coaching for all abilities and hires out wetsuits, surfboards, bodyboards and stand-up paddleboards.

FORT HOMMET

A solidly built Martello tower of red granite, **Fort Hommet** ⑳ (Apr–Oct Tue and Sat 2–4.30pm) stands on a promontory to the north of the bay and provides a panoramic view of Vazon and the whole coast. Wherever you find Napoleonic fortifications there are sure to be German defences, for the Occupation troops appreciated the skills of their predecessors in finding sites from where artillery could cover a large sweep of coast. Here, a German gun casemate has been restored as operational in 1943–5 with a full interpretation of Fort Hommet Headland.

COBO BAY

Next along is **Cobo Bay** ㉑, another fine bathing beach, particularly

Cobo Bay

Folk and Costume Museum

popular with families. As evening falls, barbecues light up along the beach, and diners gather on the terrace of the **Cobo Bay Hotel** ㉒ to watch the setting sun. The distinctive pinky-red rock along the coast here is known as Cobo granite and has long been a source of stone for buildings on the west side of the island. If you climb the steps to the top of the now-wooded quarry behind the bay, you will find the **Rocque de Guet Watchhouse and Battery**, a Napoleonic watchtower, from where there are splendid views of Vazon, Cobo and Grandes Rocques bays.

SAUMAREZ PARK

Inland from Cobo Bay, off the Route de Cobo, is **Saumarez Park** ㉓ (daylight hours; free except when special events are held here; not to be confused with Sausmarez Manor in St Martin). With a big adventure playground, vast park, tea-rooms and a nature trail linking it to nearby Cobo Bay, the park is an ideal destination for families. Garden lovers can enjoy the formal grounds surrounding the house and the Japanese walk and garden originally planted by one of the Saumarez who had served as the British ambassador to Japan. He came back with many exotic plants – plus a Japanese carpenter and gardeners to build a Japanese temple and tend the grounds. The entire property was purchased in 1938 by the States of Guernsey, and opened to the public.

FOLK AND COSTUME MUSEUM

Within the park is the National Trust of Guernsey's **Folk and Costume Museum** (www.nationaltrust-gsy.org.gg; mid-Mar–Oct daily 10am–5pm). This excellent museum, within 18th-century farm buildings grouped around a cobbled courtyard, shows life on the island as it used to be around 100 years ago. Visitors can see a reconstructed farmhouse kitchen, the town house parlour of a middle-class home and a display on childhood.

Displays in the outbuildings give an insight into the varied diet and the never-ending pattern of work involved in rural life. There are crab pots, ormering hooks, rabbit traps, pig-killing knives, carts and carriages and a Victorian mangle used by children doing the washing.

NORTHERN GUERNSEY

The grandeur of the sweeping west coast beaches gives way to smaller, more intimate bays, inlets and harbours, particularly in the northeast. The flat landscape is entirely different in character from the southern cliffs and central uplands. The west-facing coast is backed by dunes and sandy common, too poor to farm, but used as a golf course. Inland, the region is more heavily developed, with industrial complexes around St Sampson and greenhouses producing cut flowers.

AROUND LE GRAND HAVRE

Rousse Tower 24 (Apr–Oct early morning until dusk; free) which stands on the headland to the west of Le Grand

Rousse Tower

Havre, is one of a chain of 15 loop-holed towers built in the 1780s against the threat of invasion by France. It has been fully restored and contains displays on the history of Napoleonic-era fortifications on Guernsey. Perched on a small rise and visible across the bay is **Vale Church** 25 a place of worship for over 1,000 years and for pagan ritual long before that. The best bets for a swim are **Les Amarreurs Harbour** 26, a scenic beach with a small jetty and play area, or nearby **Ladies Bay** 27 where the white sands are only revealed in their glory when the tides are low.

OATLANDS VILLAGE/GUERNSEY FREESIA CENTRE

South of Le Grand Havre **Oatlands Village** 28 (www.oatlands.gg; daily 9.30am–5pm; free entrance but charges for some activities) caters for all ages. Gift shops and craft workshops are grouped around a courtyard set in converted brickworks, complete with bottle-shaped kilns. Diverse attractions over the 5-acre (2-hectare) site include an attractively landscaped mini-golf course, a Jungle House play area with a soft play zone and eight full-size trampolines, junior go-karts, Guernsey Goldsmiths, a large craft and hobbies shop, a *chocolatier* and a variety of eateries.

At the nearby **Guernsey Freesia Centre 29** (daily 10am–5pm, closed Sun in winter; free), you can see freesias at different stages of bloom and arrange to have flowers sent to friends and family at home. Flowers are dispatched daily to the UK.

L'ANCRESSE COMMON

At the very northern end of the island, from the high points on **L'Ancresse Common 30** the horizon bristles with tall circular towers and square forts, spaced at regular intervals, each one guarding a possible landing site and intended as a show of strength to deter Napoleon from planning an invasion. Far harder to spot is the oldest prehistoric site on Guernsey (and one of the earliest in Europe) hidden among the gorse and bracken on the southern edge of the common. To locate it ask a golfer for the fifth green or take the path with a sign to the site on a boulder off Les Amarreurs Road (leading to Les Amarreurs Harbour). The history is fascinating but the triangle of stones is unlikely to inspire unless you are an expert. Named **Les Fouaillages 31** this roofless burial chamber was constructed more than 6,000 years ago and only rediscovered in 1976. Two mounds rise above the golfers' 17th green: a German bunker and **La Varde**, a 40ft (12-metre) passage grave, the island's largest. In the centre of the tomb a 6ft (1.8-metre) person can stand straight and examine the huge capstones.

PEMBROKE AND L'ANCRESSE BAYS

At the north of the island the adjoining **Pembroke and L'Ancresse Bays 32** form one huge stretch of flawless beach. With white sands, water sports and clear blue waters this is arguably the island's best though it is often windy and at low tide you might run out of steam pursuing the sea hundreds of yards down the slope of sand. There are beach cafés either end

View of L'Ancresse Common

where you can sit and soak up this lovely stretch of coastline; and if it's too cool for swimming or sitting alfresco there are footpaths in either direction for a bracing walk.

The island's northern road then fringes the common and turns south. From here on, the beaches are subject to fast currents and more suited to rockpooling and birdwatching.

NORTHEAST COAST

The northeastern corner of the island is defended by the 19th-century **Fort Doyle**, truncated and modernised by the Germans. More modernity can be found in the sleek yachts at **Beaucette Marina** ㉝ an all-weather harbour blasted out of the island's bedrock. Guernsey's most atmospheric passage grave is **Le Déhus Dolmen** ㉞ (daily 9am–sunset; free) under a grassy mound right by the roadside opposite glasshouses. Not only is the dolmen perfectly preserved, with a small wooden door for an entrance, it is also dramatically lit. Look carefully and you can see a mysterious carving on one of the tomb's massive capstones: the figure of a bearded man, armed with bow and arrows, known as the Guardian of Le Déhus. The large quantity of artefacts discovered here are now in St Peter Port's Guernsey Museum.

BORDEAUX HARBOUR

Old-fashioned in comparison to Beaucette Marina, **Bordeaux Harbour** ㉟ has offered anchorage to a local fleet of boats since the Middle Ages. It's popular with fishermen and bird-watchers, and is a pleasant spot for picnics with uninterrupted views towards the islands of Herm and Sark. To the south it is overlooked by the hilltop relics of the medieval **Vale Castle**, thought to have been built on an Iron Age fort.

ST SAMPSON

The second harbour of Guernsey, the town was named after **St Sampson** who was born in Wales and moved to Brittany where he founded a monastery and became Bishop of Dol in around AD 550. He travelled from Brittany to Guernsey and is believed to have landed in the natural harbour that now bears his name. He brought Christianity to Guernsey and is said to have founded a chapel where the parish church of St Sampson now stands. Today's church was built in 1111, and originally stood on the seashore.

The former industrial hub of the island, the town has been spruced up and is home to a well-equipped modern marina. But it is still a commercial working harbour with shipyards, power station and oil tankers, and given the appeal of St Peter Port just down the road there is not a lot to detain the tourist. The main port of call for shoppers is **Ray & Scott** jewellers who specialise in diamonds and have their own diamond museum (www.rayandscott.com; Mon–Sat 9.30am–5pm; free).

HERM

This diminutive island with enticing beaches and no cars makes a wonderful day or half-day trip from Guernsey. It is just 1.5 miles (2.5km) long and 0.5-miles (0.8km) wide, with a population of 66, plus a dozen Guernsey cows. You can't own a house on Herm, play a radio in public areas or pick the flowers; and the only vehicles are those used by residents for essential business purposes. Visitors come to this little paradise for the scenery, the swimming, the walking and the birdlife. It's also a favourite of foodies who come over from Guernsey for lunch or on the early evening boat to enjoy freshly caught lobster or Herm-farmed oysters. The best way to enjoy all this peace is to walk around the island. Unlike the other islands bikes (as well as cars) are banned on Herm, except for local children.

⊘ BECOMING A LOCAL

If you fall in love with Guernsey, and fancy living here, you will need deep pockets. A glance at any estate agent's window will reveal that there are two types of property on the market: reasonably priced accommodation and the phenomenally expensive. One two-bedroom apartment may be priced at £350,000, whilst its identical neighbour costs £1 million. The reason is that the cheaper apartment can only be bought by a Guernsey native, whilst the millionaire's property is for sale on the open market. By this means Guernsey controls migration to the islands, which would otherwise be flooded by tax exiles.

Ferries take 20 minutes from St Peter Port and depart eight times a day in July and August, with a reduced service off-season. Tickets can be bought from the Travel Trident Ferries kiosk on the harbour (www.traveltrident.com) or from the boat crew as you board.

HERM HARBOUR

At high tide ferries dock in **Herm harbour 36**, while at low water passengers disembark at the Rosaire Steps before making their way along the track to the harbour. The long-established **White House Hotel 37**, overlooking gardens and beach, is a country house hotel with an old-fashioned charm and sense of decorum. A stay here is an escape from the 21st century – there are no televisions or telephones in the bedrooms and no clocks on the walls. Drunken quarrymen used to be incarcerated in the tiny gaol by the hotel's tennis courts, said to be Britain's smallest gaol. Any troublemakers today are shipped back to Guernsey and the prison is used to store lawnmowers.

The path going north passes the **Mermaid Tavern** (see page 111), the social hub of the island. Beyond it, **Fisherman's Beach** at low tide reveals weed-covered crates in which Herm's oysters are grown. For swimming and sunbathing there are better beaches on the east side of the island. The first main landmark on the northwards route is a tiny **cemetery**

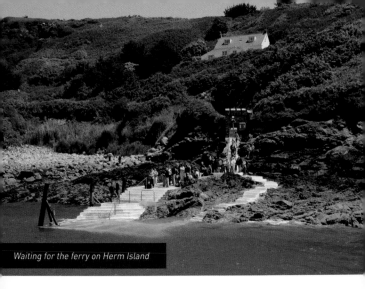
Waiting for the ferry on Herm Island

containing two graves and an almost indecipherable inscription; local legend has it that this is the grave of a mother and child who died of cholera in the early 19th century, buried here by the crew of a passing ship.

HERM COMMON

In the north of the island Herm Common has over 450 species of wild flowers, among them prickly burnet roses, sea holly, foxglove and wild thyme. Neolithic tombs, often indistinguishable from natural scatters of rock, lie scattered around the common.

The needle-shaped monument at the northernmost point of the island marks the position of one of the island's more famous dolmens, called the **Pierre aux Rats**. When quarrymen destroyed the massive grave, the local seamen were incensed at the loss of such an important landmark and navigational aid, so the obelisk was erected in its place.

SHELL BEACH AND BELVOIR BAY

Along the northeast coast lies the dazzling white, Caribbean-like expanse of **Shell Beach** ㊳. It consists almost entirely of shells, though most have been pulverised to fragments of sand by centuries of wave action. Each tide brings in a new crop of delicate pink, yellow and luminescent shells to keep beachcombers happy. As you explore, however, you will discover that Shell Beach is by no means unique: all the island's beaches have a large amount of shells, as does the island soil.

Further south **Belvoir Bay** has a smaller but more sheltered beach, and has lovely views of Sark and (on a clear day) France. It is perfect for swimming but the sands can get crowded in summer.

SOUTHERN CLIFFS

From Belvoir Bay a path heads south along the undulating (and at times steep) cliff path, which encircles the island and gives access to some excellent birdwatching points. The best

⦿ POST-WAR HERM

During World War II, the island escaped fortification, and was largely left to decay, so that the first post-war tenant spent a small fortune restoring the island farms. Even so, much remained to be done when Peter and Jenny Wood became tenants in 1949. The story of how they fell in love with Herm and worked to create the thriving but unspoilt island of today, based on the twin pillars of tourism and farming, is told in the late Jenny Wood's delightful book, *Herm, Our Island Home*, available from the gift shop at Herm Harbour.

times are the spring and autumn migration periods, when the Channel Islands serve as a feeding ground for birds of passage. The cliffs attract nesting puffins and fulmars. In spring and early summer you can take a two-hour puffin-watching kayak tour (www.outdoorguernsey.co.uk) starting at Shell Beach, led by expert kayak instructors who are very knowledgeable about the puffins' routines.

Also keep an eye out for the grey seals and bottlenose and common dolphins that have made their home in the northern rocky outcrop called The Humps.

LE MANOIR

An alternative to going south along the cliff path is to head up the steep track to the huddle of granite houses at the centre

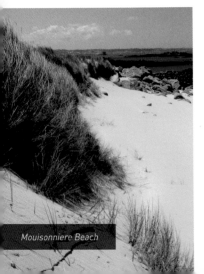

Mouisonniere Beach

of the island on the brow of the hill. Le Manoir is the village where the islanders live. Here there is an unobtrusive power station, a workshop, cottages, primary school, and the tenant's home. What appears to be a medieval keep was built in the 19th century by Prince Blücher von Wahlstatt, a wealthy and eccentric German aristocrat. He fell in love with the place in 1890 and bought the island lease. The prince introduced many trees to the island

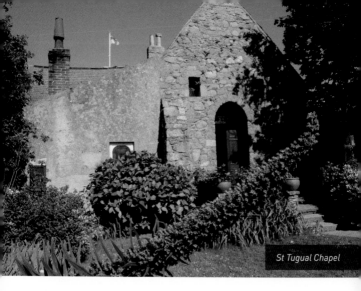

St Tugual Chapel

along with a colony of wallabies, which bred successfully but have since vanished.

A subsequent tenant of the island was the novelist, Sir Compton Mackenzie, best remembered for Whisky Galore (1928), who lived here from 1920 until he retired to the neighbouring island of Jethou.

ST TUGUAL

The enchanting little Norman chapel dedicated to the enigmatic St Tugual has a pint-sized bell-tower and a pretty garden with a memorial to Peter and Jenny Wood, former tenants of the island (see page 65). Rumour has it that the saint was a Welsh woman who accompanied St Magloire to Guernsey and Herm in the 6th century, and her memory was perpetuated by the building of the shrine. The Wood family restored the chapel and it is used for a service at 10am most Sundays.

SARK

Victor Hugo considered Sark to be *'la plus belle'* of the Channel Islands. It is still a peaceful little island, remaining in its famous time-warp, with the atmosphere of Victorian England. The island has a population of 600 and the head of its government (or Chief Pleas) holds the ancient feudal title of Seigneur. There are no tarmac roads and the only motorized vehicles are the tractors, the ambulance and four-wheel mobility scooters.

Sark's constitution dates back to 1563, when Helier de Carteret was granted sovereignty over the island in return for maintaining a militia, whose chief task was to keep the island free of the pirates who had been using Sark as a base from which to harass English shipping. Helier took 40 Jerseymen with him to colonise the uninhabited island. He divided Sark into 40 parcels of land and granted perpetual tenancy to the occupants in return for their help in defending the island. These tenements, as they are known, have remained virtually unchanged. The feudal form of government set up in Elizabeth I's reign prevailed right up until 2008 when the island held its first general election and Sark became Europe's newest democracy.

FERRIES TO SARK

Ferries to the island are run by the Isle of Sark Shipping Company (www.sarkshippingcompany.com, tel: 01481-724 059) and depart from St Peter Port on Guernsey, with several sailings a day in season. The crossing time is around 50 minutes. Book ahead in the summer months when Sark is very popular with families. If you decide to stay on the island there are hotels, guest houses or self-catering options.

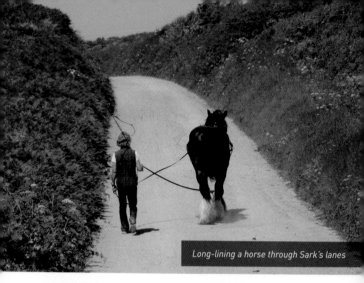

Long-lining a horse through Sark's lanes

BRECQHOU AND THE BARCLAY BROTHERS

The ferry passes south of Herm before swinging northwards past the rocky islet of **Brecqhou** ③. This island's tenement was sold by Dame Sybil Hathaway, the most famous ruler of Sark, in 1929 for £3,000 and purchased in 1993 for a reputed £2 million as a private tax haven by the reclusive billionaire Barclay brothers, best known as owners of the Telegraph Media Group and The Ritz. The tycoon twins created a massive mock-Gothic castle on the island, complete with walls, turrets and a helipad. You can't miss it as the ferry swings to the north of Sark.

In 2008, against the wishes of the majority of the islanders, the brothers instigated the first full election on Sark. Up until then the Chief Pleas (Sark's government) had mainly comprised members who had inherited their seats under the island's 450-year-old feudal system of government. When the majority of voters rejected the Barclay brothers' preferred

Maseline Harbour

candidates and their manager in Sark lost his seat in the new Chief Pleas office, they withdrew their £5-million annual investment in Sark and temporarily closed down their businesses on Sark including two hotels, a pub and shops, and over 100 Sark workers were laid off.

The bitter feud continues. The Barclay brothers own around a quarter of Sark and continue to seek the full de-feudalisation of the island. In 2012 the UK Minister of State for Justice, Lord McNally, informed the brothers that the UK would not let them turn the tiny island into a 'company town'. In 2015 the brothers announced the closure of all four of their hotels and other holiday businesses in Sark for the foreseeable future.

ARRIVAL IN SARK

The ferry comes in close beneath Sark's towering cliffs, past rocks where cormorants and shags launch themselves on fishing flights. At **Maseline Harbour** ❹⓿ ferries are met by a team of carters who take passengers' luggage to their accommodation. Sark's pettiest port, backed by a tiny shingle beach, is **Creux Harbour**, to the south, linked by tunnels through the cliffs and dotted with colourful fishing boats and smart yachts.

To reach the main village, you can either hop on the 'toast rack' – an open-sided tractor-drawn cart, which makes light of the short but steep haul up Harbour Hill – or take the pretty woodland footpath which runs alongside the road. The morning arrival of a flood of day trippers can mar this paradise, but if you head away from the village, tranquillity is assured.

GETTING AROUND

Sark is so small you can explore it by bike in a day, preferably with a map. Bikes can be hired cheaply from **Avenue Cycle Hire** on **The Avenue** (www.avenuecyclessark.co.uk). In season it's best to book in advance. There are some steep hills but pedalling is otherwise easy going. To explore some of the bays and rocky shores you have to leave the bike (no need to lock up) and continue on foot. If you're scrambling around the coastline do be aware of the state of the tide.

For the less energetic there are Sark's famous horse-drawn carriages which wait patiently at the top of the hill to take visitors on tours (approximately £10 per person for an hour). There are now more than 70 tractors, which are used for agricultural purposes, cargo deliveries and by the doctor. The ambulance is still the back end of a conventional ambulance, towed by a tractor.

BIG SARK

Sark's main road, **The Avenue**, is lined by souvenir shops, grocery stores, bike-hire outlets and café/bistros that are open all day. Note that although there is a bank, Sark has no ATMs. Most of the shops and restaurants take credit and debit cards, and some operate a cash-back system for up to £50. At the far end, beside the tourist information office, is the two-cell island prison, built to hold drunken quarry workers. Today the Sarkese locals are elected by the Chief Pleas to become the Connétable (special constable) who oversees the gaol.

St Peter's Church

The nearby **St Peter's Church**, built in 1820, has a pew reserved for prisoners, identifiable by a crossed keys design on the cushion covers. The simple building has stained-glass windows of various saints, including St Magloire, who came from Dol in Brittany in 565 to found a monastery on Sark. The monastery flourished, supporting 62 monks and serving as a school for the children of the Breton nobility, until marauding Viking pirates destroyed the buildings and killed the monks.

Continuing north you pass a stone building which houses the **Assembly Room** where the Chief Pleas' meetings take place four times a year. Sark's feudal state came to an end in 2008 when the Chief Pleas was reformed and Sark held its first election. Although Sark is no longer a feudal state and the powers of the Seigneur are much eroded, he still holds the island in perpetuity for the Crown, sits in the Court of Chief Pleas and pays the Queen an annual rent of £1.79.

LA SEIGNEURIE GARDENS

A little further north, you will be sharing the road with horses and carriages heading to and from **La Seigneurie Gardens** ❹ (01481-832 208; www.laseigneuriegardens. com; Easter–Oct daily 10am–6pm; guided tours every Wed at 11.30am, booking essential).

The sheltered **walled gardens** are packed with colourful flowers and shrubs, including climbing roses and exotic plants such as the Australian Bottlebrush and New Zealand Tea Tree that flourish in the frost-free island environment. Beyond the walled garden are fruit and vegetables, which supply the on-site brasserie and a Sensory Garden whose medicinal, scented and edible plants are aimed to stimulate all five senses. The house itself (not open to the public) is no less exotic than the gardens, with the Dutch gables of its Victorian wing added to the original house of 1732 and a large watchtower built, so it is said, for sending signals to Guernsey in 1854.

Displays in the renovated chapel tell the history of Sark's Seigneurs and the Seigneurie. To the rear of the house is

⊙ WILD SARK

Sark's isolated position brings a wealth of wildlife. Among the species you are likely to see along the rugged coast are puffins, shags, guillemots, razorbills and oyster catchers. For the best sitings bring your binoculars and take a three-hour trip around the island with local fisherman, George Guille (tel: 01481-832 107). You will sail past spectacular rock formations and visit caves with deep clear water, secret beaches and coves that are only accessible by sea. Trips must be pre-booked.

One of Sark's many ancient laws forbids the shooting of seagulls, because of the guidance the birds' cries gave mariners when the wind dropped and their nesting rocks and headlands vanished into sudden sea mists. Until the mid-19th century, when it was finally conceded that another war with France was unlikely, the way into Sark's harbours was a closely guarded secret.

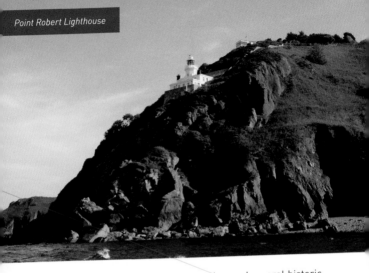

the Battery, where a cider apple crusher and several historic cannons are displayed alongside an ornate tower, and a turreted 18th-century dovecote. Until relatively recently one of the Seigneur's sole privileges was to keep pigeons and doves, which fed freely and with impunity on the crops of the tenants.

AROUND THE ISLAND

Sark comes into its element when you leave the village, with glorious countryside and sheer cliffs almost everywhere you go. Most of the beaches entail an adventurous scramble down the hillside – tricky if you have a bike, but it's all part of the Sark experience.

PORT DU MOULIN AND LIGHTHOUSE

A short way along the track north of La Seigneurie is a left turn that leads down through woods to **Port du Moulin** (once the site of a watermill), with fine coastal scenery. Just before you get to the beach, look out for the artificial 'Window in the Rock', a square hole perhaps cut through the cliff to allow carts to descend to the beach and gather *vraic*, or seaweed, used for fertilising the Seigneur's fields and garden. At the northern tip of the island **L'Eperquerie Common**, is named after the poles *(perques)* once erected here for drying fish.

On the east coast Sark's **lighthouse** was built in 1912 and automated in 1993. It stands halfway down the cliff into which it nestles and its platform, accessed via a flight of 165 steps, offers superb views of Maseline Harbour. On a clear day you can see all the way to France.

In Sark's southeast corner lie the best beaches and some splendid cliff scenery from the spectacular rocky spines of the Hog's Back and Pointe Derrible. **Dixcart Bay**, a fine sandy spot for bathing when the tide is out, is reached via Stocks Hotel, along a beautiful woodland path leading to the valley bottom.

On the west side of the island the **Pilcher Monument,** on the high cliffs above the harbour of Havre Gosselin, commemorates Joseph Pilcher, a London merchant who lost his life with four others while sailing to Guernsey in a storm in 1868. This was just one of many shipwrecks.

LA COUPÉE

The vertiginous land bridge known as **La Coupée** ㊷ links Big Sark and Little Sark and is Sark's most famous landmark. A roadway tops the knife-edge ridge, some 10ft (3 metres) wide – you can easily take

Gold Post Box

Sark's only post box was painted gold in 2012 to celebrate local resident Carl Hester's gold medal win for his part in the British Olympic Dressage team.

a bike across but a notice warns cyclists to dismount while crossing. To either side there is an almost sheer drop of 260ft (80 metres) straight to the sea. Crossing La Coupée was once extremely hazardous and schoolchildren had to crawl across the causeway in high winds, but the path was made good with concrete and handrails in 1945 by German prisoners of war. The steep flight of steps leading down from the north end of La Coupée to the lovely **Grand Grève** beach on the right was closed after a landslide in 2010. Two years on, the steps were repaired by volunteers and the fabulous bay is once again accessible.

LITTLE SARK

Beyond La Coupée **Little Sark** is even more peaceful than the main island. Enjoy the views of neighbouring islands as you

La Coupée

follow the sunken lane to La Sablonnerie, a charming hotel with restaurant and tea gardens. A left turn here brings you to the tall granite chimney pots and ruins of Sark's **silver mines**, growing out of the wild bracken and brambles. Silver and copper were discovered on Sark in the 1830s and Cornish miners were brought over to work it. But no viable quantities were found, ten miners were drowned in 1845, and two years later, when the galleries collapsed and flooded, the ill-fated mining company went bankrupt.

Few make it as far as the southern tip of Little Sark and **Venus Pool**, a large natural rock pool at the base of the nearby cliffs. The 10ft (3-metre) -deep pool is uncovered for 2.5 hours either side of a low tide and visitors frequently fail to find it (ask locally about the tides and check the way). When the grass runs out and gives way to bare granite, cairns mark the best route. Reaching the pool involves a scramble, but it's a lovely spot to swim.

ALDERNEY

The island of Alderney has largely escaped mainstream tourism and remains quiet and unspoilt, with a friendly and relaxed atmosphere and a refreshing lack of bureaucracy. It certainly feels very different from Jersey or Guernsey – it is much more sparsely populated and feels quite remote even though it is only 8 miles (13km) from France. Despite its small size (3.5 miles/5.5km x 1.5 miles/2.5km) there are many miles of footpaths around the island, making it a haven for walkers and birdwatchers.

Visitors also come for the fine sandy beaches, the sailing, the restaurants and the watering holes. The islanders have a reputation for conviviality and there is a definite emphasis on taking time out to eat, drink and be merry. If you're tired

Alderney Society Museum

of walking Alderney's wind-blasted cliffs in a squall, sitting in a warm pub is the best thing to do. The pubs are more like clubs – full of character and characters, and the natural place to be on an island that offers few places of entertainment. Alderney stole a march on Guernsey by being the first to allow publicans to open on Sundays.

Alderney's character differs somewhat from the other islands, partly because it was deliberately depopulated during World War II and used as a forced labour camp. The island was massively fortified by the Germans; relics of the Occupation can be seen along the coastline.

There are cars to hire and organised island tours but the island is best suited to those who like getting around by pedal power or on foot. A hiker can circle the island in a day.

ST ANNE

Just a few minutes' walk from **Alderney Airport 43**, the island's capital. **St Anne 44** (referred to by locals simply as 'town') is an attractive maze of cobbled streets and pastel-coloured houses. **Victoria Street** is the main shopping street, with some delightfully quirky little shops. **The Alderney Visitor and Wildlife Information Centre** is a good source of information on island walks. Just to the south the Victorian **St Anne's Church**, designed by Sir George Gibert Scott, is so big that it's known as 'the Cathedral of the Channel Islands'.

Alderney Society Museum

In the High Street, perpendicular to Victoria Street, the **Alderney Society Museum** (www.alderneysociety.org; Apr–Oct Mon–Fri 10am–noon and 2.30–4.30pm, Sat–Sun 10am–noon), occupies an 18th-century schoolhouse and covers the fascinating story of this little island from the Stone Age to World War II. Exhibits include first-hand accounts of Nazi soldiers and the slaves transported here from all over Europe to turn the island into an impregnable fortress. Like all the Channel Islands Alderney has a history of shipwrecks, and the museum displays some absorbing finds salvaged from an Elizabethan warship, *Makeshift*, which was wrecked off the coast and discovered in 1977 by a fisherman.

BRAYE HARBOUR

From the centre of St Anne's it's just a few minutes' walk down the hill to **Braye Harbour** ⑮ and the great sandy sweep of **Braye Bay**. Protecting the beach and harbour is the massive **Braye Breakwater**, often pounded by heavy seas (walkers along the wall should be aware of sudden swamping by breaking waves). When the French began constructing a naval

The Alderney Spike Girls

The distinctive blonde hedgehog is extremely rare but on little Alderney there is a population of around 1,000. The creamy-coloured flea-free creatures, with beady button-black eyes, have a rare recessive gene. They have been breeding here since a couple of them were released in the 1960s – allegedly from a Harrods shopping bag.

Alderney Railway carriage

harbour at Cherbourg, alarm bells rang in the Admiralty, and the British government suddenly decided it was urgent to create two breakwaters to protect ships at Braye, as well as on Guernsey and Jersey. The intention was to convert Braye harbour into a huge naval base. But only the western wall was built, completed in 1847. Battered by massive waves, part of the breakwater was abandoned and now lies submerged beneath the waves.

Before the Royal Navy discovered Braye it was a busy little port, much frequented by smugglers and privateers. The cellars of the 18th century houses near the port were used for storing contraband. Today these houses are bars and restaurants.

ALDERNEY RAILWAY

The Alderney Railway is one of the oldest in the British Isles, constructed in the 1840s by the British government to convey stone from Mannez Quarry to build the breakwater and the forts. The first official passengers were Queen Victoria and Prince Albert, who were carried in 1854 in a horse-drawn tender. At weekends and on bank holidays in season visitors can take a trip in a diesel-powered railcar or one of two 1938 London underground carriages, from Braye Road to Mannez Station (or vice versa), a journey of 15 minutes.

THE NORTHEAST

A circular road hugs the northeast coast, forming a loop from Braye back to St Anne. **Fort Albert** is the first in the chain of 12 fortresses encircling the island, designed in the 1840s and 1850s. Most were never garrisoned and some have now been converted into private flats and holiday apartments, while others remain in a decayed and dangerous state. Fort Albert is perhaps the finest of them all, and is well positioned to defend Braye Harbour.

SAYE AND CORBLETS BAYS

North of Fort Albert Saye Bay (pronounced 'Soy') is an idyllic horseshoe-shaped white-sand beach between rocky headlands. Children love leaping off the rocks here – and in summer it's popular with campers from the island's only campsite just over the

⊙ FLYING TO ALDERNEY

From Guernsey the easiest, although not the cheapest, way to get to Alderney is to hop across by plane. It takes just 20 minutes and costs around £80–120 return. Aurigny Air Services (www.aurigny.com) operate a daily service to Alderney with their 19-seat aircraft. Waves (www.flywaves.gg) provide an air taxi to the island that carries up to seven passengers. Alderney Airport, opened in 1935, was the first officially recognised airport of the Channel Islands. The small Terminal was built in the 1960s and has changed little over the years. Ferries to Alderney from Guernsey are very limited. Manche Iles Express (www.manche-iles-express.com) operates a high-speed ferry at weekends from April to September and the slower Lady Maris II (www.alderneygiftbox.com) only runs on Thursdays).

Longis Bay

dunes. The next beach along is the delightful **Corblets Bay**, with clean sands and shallow waters. This is the best beach on the island for surfing and body-boarding.

MANNEZ QUARRY AND LIGHTHOUSE

Evidence of quarrying activity lies all around the north-eastern tip of the island at **Mannez Quarry**, close to the railway station terminus. Above the quarry stands the large and sinister naval direction-finder tower, built by the Germans and known locally as **The Odeon**. To the east the **Mannez Hide** is a secluded spot overlooking a pond with nine species of resident dragonfly. On the coast **Mannez Lighthouse** was built in 1912 to aid vessels along this treacherous stretch of coast. It now has LED lights and is controlled from Trinity House, Harwich. The Alderney Wildlife Trust organises tours from May to September (tel: 01481-822 333; Sun at 3pm).

AROUND LONGIS BAY

Continuing around the coast, **Longis Bay** is a broad crescent of white sand offering safe bathing and fine views. Additional shelter is provided by the massive concrete anti-tank wall that was partially constructed by the Germans. At the far end of Longis Bay, an attractive château-like building, known locally as **The Nunnery**, stands on the site of Alderney's Roman fort.

Just to the north, **Longis Nature Reserve** and **Longis Pond and Hide** are favourite spots for ornithologists.

SOUTH OF THE ISLAND

The south coast is mainly dramatic cliff walks, with almost sheer cliffs westward all the way to Hannaine Bay. This is Alderney at its most beautiful and ruggedly spectacular. Footpaths among thrift, sea campion and broom follow the line of the clifftops and you may see birds of prey soaring in the updraughts. Take binoculars for spectacular views of gannetries. South of the airport **Telegraph Bay** was previously a favourite retreat for swimming and sunbathing when the tide was out but the steps down fell into disrepair and the beach is sadly inaccessible.

Rounding the headland the offshore islands of **Les Etacs** and distant **Ortac** teem with over 11,000 gannets, a colony which grew from a single pair that nested here in 1940. Boat trips are available in season. North of Hannaine Bay a causeway leads out to **Fort Clonque**, a Victorian fort that has been converted by the Landmark Trust into holiday accommodation (see page 140). You can only access the fort when the tide is out. The next fort up is **Fort Tourgis**, a Victorian fortification adapted by the German forces. The **Cambridge Battery** has been restored and is the only British fortification on the island which is open to the public.

Burhou Island

A couple of miles offshore, the tiny island of Burhou provides a refuge for breeding sea birds, including more than 120 breeding pairs of puffins. The island has a closed season from mid-March to 1 August to avoid disturbance to breeding seabirds. Serious birdwatchers can arrange to stay overnight in a basic hut during the months that the island is open.

Fun on the beach at Vazon Bay

WHAT TO DO

With a wide range of outdoor activities on offer, beautiful scenery and interesting wildlife, there are no shortage of things to do should you tire of Guernsey's many beaches. It's also a great place to take the kids on holiday, with plenty of child-friendly attractions.

SPORTS AND OUTDOOR PURSUITS

Spectacular cliff-top paths, beautiful bays for water sports and clear blue seas for fishing provide endless ways to enjoy the great outdoors in Guernsey. Along with established activities such as golf and sailing, sports enthusiasts can now try their hand at abseiling, coasteering and other adventure activities.

SURFING AND WINDSURFING

The rollers on Guernsey are not comparable to those on Jersey, but with the right conditions you can find surf on the island's west coast at Vazon Bay. The Guernsey Surf School which is based there (www.guernseysurfschool.co.uk) offers lessons and courses. Courses take place daily from July to September and are open to eight years and older, and they also run Summer Camps. The Sailing Trust Windsurfing, located on the Castle Emplacement in St Peter Port, offer windsurf lessons.

SCUBA DIVING

Conditions are good for scuba diving with clean (and cold) waters, good visibility and plentiful marine life. The Blue Dolphins Sub Aqua Club (www.bdsac.org.gg) offers a range of diving experiences, including shipwrecks. Dive Guernsey (www.diveguernsey. co.uk) organises courses to explore the reefs and caves around

Sailboats, St Peter

Sark, Herm and Alderney as well. The clear waters are also excellent for snorkelling and swimming.

SAILING

A steady breeze blows around the coast making Guernsey popular among yachting enthusiasts, but inexperienced sailors should beware of the tides and currents.

The Guernsey Sailing Trust (www.sailingtrust.org.gg) caters for all ages and offers a wide variety of courses, including dinghy, powerboat and windsurf lessons. The Guernsey Yacht Club at St Peter Port has full marina services, welcomes visiting yachtsmen and offers dinghy training and a wide range of boating activities. Skippered boat charter can be organised through Guernsey Boating (www.guernseyboating.com).

The Model Yacht Pond on Castle Emplacement in St Peter Port is ideal for model boat and yacht sailing or racing and is also used for beginners' sailing lessons.

ADVENTURE SPORTS

You can abseil on the west coast as the sun sets, climb the cliffs in the morning light or roll down the hill inside a giant transparent plastic ball (zorbing). Coasteering routes enable punters to experience the exhilaration of sea-level traversing, rock scrambling, kayaking, jumping and swimming in gullies and caves. You just come equipped with a swimming costume, a good pair of trainers, shorts or tracksuit, and a change of clothes for later. Outdoor Guernsey (www.outdoorguernsey.co.uk) hire out kayaks and operate sea kayak and coasteering trips on Guernsey year-round. During the summer, they also hire out kayaks on Herm. To explore the cave systems and beautiful wild coastline of Sark, contact Adventure Sark (www.adventuresark.com).

SWIMMING

Guernsey alone has 27 bays. If you're planning on spending time on the beach bear in mind the tides and the wind. Some

⊙ BOATS AND BIRDS

Cruising around the Guernsey coast, chartering a speed boat, spotting dolphins or seals, landing mackerel or sea bass and hopping across to islands are among the many boating options. Take a leisurely afternoon cruise around the east and south coast of Guernsey on board the Sark Belle (www.sark-shippingcompany.com), which captures spectacular coastline and beautiful bays whilst spotting puffins, oystercatchers, gannets, guillemots and other breeding seabirds. Representatives of Guernsey RSPB will be on board to provide a commentary, helping you to identify different bird species. Island RIB voyages (www.islandribvoyages.com) offer adrenaline-fuelled trips in rigid inflatable boats, exploring bays, caves and islands.

On Sark a boat trip is the best way to explore the rugged coast, caves and birdlife. On Alderney there are seasonal boat trips to see the puffin colony and gannetries; and from April to July you can join puffin-watching kayak trips from Shell Beach on Herm (www.outdoorguernsey.co.uk).

Gannet colony on
Les Etacs

of the pretty little bays in the south are only revealed at low tide, while beaches in the north are exposed to chilly winds. Watch out too for incoming tides when the water gallops across the sands – Guernsey has one of the largest tidal ranges in the world. If you are used to indoor pools or swimming in the Mediterranean, the Channel Island waters will feel on the cool side. Most beachgoers do no more than paddle, leaving the seas delightfully crowd-free for serious swimmers. The beaches are washed twice daily by the tides and the waters are clear, but beware of strong currents and rip tides.

FISHING

With their varied coastlines, offshore reefs and clear waters the Channel Islands are ideal locations for sea anglers, especially from mid-summer to the end of autumn. The Bailiwick of Guernsey has about one fifth of all British shore records. Depending on the tides you could be bank fishing for turbot, bass and brill, wrecking for cod, conger and ling or reef fishing for pollack, bream or bass. Late summer or early autumn are ideal for shore fishing for bream, bass, sole, red mullet, triggerfish, plaice, wrasse, conger and garfish, while autumn to early winter is best for wrasse and mullet. Commercial operators include Out the Blue charters (www.boatfishing.net) for groups of 10–12 with a choice of wreck fishing, deep sea reef fishing, bank fishing or bass angling. Alderney has an international reputation as a shore fishing centre where record-breaking ballan wrasse and monster grey mullet are landed.

Rock pools are a haven for crabs, shrimps and devil fish. At strictly enforced times of the year you can seek out the ormer, valued by locals for their meat and by tourists for their fine mother-of-pearl interior shells. At very low tide you can sprinkle salt on the key-holed burrows of razor fish, wait for them to pop up (they will think the tide is in), then pull them from their holes. The clams are slightly chewy but can be delicious if cooked correctly, ideally steamed with wine, garlic and herbs. The best beaches for collecting the clams are L'Ancresse Bay and any of the west coast beaches on a low spring tide.

WALKING

Walking opportunities are plentiful, from dramatic rugged cliffs to the leafy lanes of the interior. The most spectacular and challenging walk is the cliff path starting at St Peter Port and ending at desolate Pleinmont Point. The cliffs are around 320ft (100 metres) high and afford wonderful views of the tiny coves below and the waves crashing on to the rocks. The path dips down to villages where cafés and pubs provide happy distractions en route. The walk can either be done in its entirety over a long day, or in separate shorter sections at a gentler pace. With a local bus timetable you can work out when and where to be picked up

Fishing on the Net

For information on species you can catch in Guernsey and where and when to fish for them, visit www.fishing-guernsey.co.uk. It also covers charter boat hire, tackle and bait shops.

Coastal footpath near Petit

and need not retrace your steps. The scenery is best in spring when wild flowers are in bloom and birds come ashore to nest.

An extensive programme of themed walks with accredited guides runs from April to September. Guides are enthusiastic and dedicated, and provide a remarkable range of themed walks. Information is available from the Guernsey Information Centre, which also provides a free walking map of Guernsey and details of Tasty Walks, a series of 20 self-guided walks designed for all ages and abilities, and punctuated by plenty of cafés, restaurants and beachside kiosks. The walks can be downloaded at www.visitguernsey.com; a full audio transcript is available, as are interactive maps.

During the Spring and Autumn Walking Festivals, guided walks focus on different aspects of Guernsey's natural beauty and heritage, with around 40 walks to choose from. *Walking on Guernsey* (published by Cicerone Guides) is an excellent booklet describing 25 walks on Guernsey, Alderney, Sark and Herm. The most detailed maps of the islands are the Ordnance Survey-style Bailiwick of Guernsey (1:15,000) or the Perry's official guide. When exploring the coast, watch out for extreme tidal movement, one of the largest recorded in the world. Beaches can disappear rapidly, so it's best to plan with an abundance of caution. And don't forget comfortable shoes, binoculars and sunblock.

Alderney has 50 miles (80km) of footpaths, across commons, cliffs and beaches. The Alderney Wildlife Trust organises informative guided walks from May to September, ranging from history and heritage to bird watching and bat walks, plus useful leaflets on self-guided walks. During Alderney Wildlife Week in May guided walks explore the wide range of habitat and species on the island, including the unusual blonde hedgehogs. The small island of Sark is ideal for walking, as is its neighbouring island Herm, although there you have no other choice. Sark Guided Walks (www.sarkguidedwalks.co.uk) offer three options led by Beth, a very informative and experienced local.

Every year adventurous locals walk all the way around Guernsey in a day for charity. It is a 48.5 mile (78-km) -hike, beginning at 5am. Visitors are welcome to take up the challenge. And for something even more challenging there is The Channel Island Way, a 110-mile (176km) walking route incorporating the best coastal walks in Jersey, Guernsey, Alderney, Sark and Herm. Serious ramblers can do the whole route in a fortnight (including the island-hops on ferries or boats). Obviously you don't have to do the whole route, nor do you have to be a super-fit walker. The routes on the main islands are divided into sections of 2–4 miles (3–6km), with a car park, bus stop and café at each end.

BIRDWATCHING

Guernsey has its own branch of the Royal Society for the Protection of Birds (RSPB), which welcomes members and non-members on their local, two-hour guided walks (for more information, visit www.rspbguernsey.co.uk). Expect to see oystercatchers, shags, cormorants, gulls, egrets, fulmars, razorbills, guillemots, puffins, and many more. The smaller islands are favourites for birdwatchers, particularly the puffins and gannets on Alderney. On Herm there are puffin-watching boat trips and on Sark you can take bird-watching tours with a local fisherman.

CYCLING

Fit cyclists can forget the car on Guernsey and use pedal power to enjoy the scenery. No distance on Guernsey is too far to cycle, though you may find the amount of traffic you encounter off-putting, not to mention the local 4x4s which leave you little space on the narrow country lanes. Outdoor Guernsey (www.outdoorguernsey.co.uk) offer three-hour guided tours, each visiting off-the-beaten-track attractions and starting at different locations.

The most pleasant roads for cycling are the *Ruettes Tranquilles* (Quiet Lanes) where pedestrians, cyclists and horse-riders have priority over cars, and motorists are meant to slow down to a sedate 15mph (24kmh). For information on cycle hire in Guernsey see page 116.

Cyclists taking in the view from Sark across to Brecqhou

On Sark, where cars are banned, bikes are a popular way of getting around. Unlike Sark, Herm does not allow cycling.

GOLF

The number one golf course is the Royal Guernsey Golf Club (www.royalguernsey-golfclub.com), a seaside course by L'Ancresse Bay in the north of the island where visitors need to produce a handicap certificate from a recognised club. But all are welcome at the 18-hole La Grande Mare at Vazon Bay (www.lagrande-mare.com) and the 9-hole par 3 course designed by Tony Jacklin at St Pierre Park Hotel in St Peter Port (www.stpierrepark.co.uk).

On Alderney the 9-hole Alderney Golf Club (www.alderneygolfclub.com) is a scenic and testing course, with fine views of France.

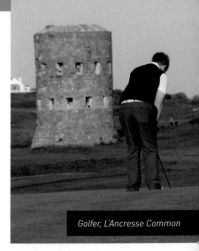
Golfer, L'Ancresse Common

HORSE RIDING

The long-established Melrose Farm Riding School (tel: 01481-257 267) in Castel caters for all ages and standards. It has an all-weather arena overlooking the west coast and takes rides to Vazon beach.

On Alderney you can explore scenic cliffs and country paths on horseback and, from October to March, beaches too. To book a ride, contact Jill Moore (email: bjmoore65@yahoo.co.uk or text on 07781-421 325).

SHOPPING

Guernsey is not a full member of the EU, and VAT is non-existent. However this doesn't mean that the shops are packed with bargains. Many of them put up prices for 'freight surcharge'. Moreover not all goods are VAT-free as some shops retain VAT on goods that have come from the UK. The best buys are wines, spirits and tobacco, and to a lesser extent cosmetics, perfume and jewellery which are all duty-free.

ST PETER PORT

The main shopping centre is St Peter Port, particularly the High Street and its extension, Le Pollet and Lower Pollet where individual, locally-owned shops alternate with the familiar High Street names. Jewellers predominate, selling everything from silver milk cans to gold chain by the yard. Market Square is at its liveliest on Friday mornings in season when stalls are set up with crafts, local produce and ethnic street food.

AROUND THE ISLAND

Jewellery outlets are dotted around the island. **Bruce Russell & Son Gold and Silversmiths** (www.bruce-russell.com) at Le Gron in St Saviours make beautiful items from gold, silver and platinum, including candlesticks, goblets, spoons, caskets and the traditional Guernsey loving cup. The family business has been going strong since 1887 and has the bonus of an 8-acre (3-hectare) award-winning garden and a brasserie and tea room (see page 109). Award-winning jeweller **Catherine Best** (www.catherinebest. com) runs a family business operating from an historic windmill in St Martin and is known for her diverse designs, often styled from rare, fabulously coloured gemstones. Most of the designs are limited editions. At **Guernsey Pearl** (www.

Farmers' Market

The Farmers' Market at Sausmarez Manor on Saturday mornings is well worth a diversion. It has a wonderful range of local produce from Guernsey crabs, beef and cheese to handmade crafts, antiques and plants.

guernseypearl.com), opposite Fort Grey on the west coast, the pearls come from the Far East but are made up here. Visitors can watch the pearl stringing and purchase jewellery.

A cluster of attractions in the north of the island are ideal for rainy days. **Oatlands Village** (see page 58) provides a convenient one-stop shop for all sorts of hand-made items, from chocolates to perfume bottles. Close by are

Catherine Best necklace

the **Guernsey Freesia Centre** and **Guernsey Candles** where you can watch wax being dyed and moulded, and children can make their own candle.

ENTERTAINMENT

Visit the tourist office or pick up a copy of *The Guernsey Press* for details of what's on. Guernsey's premier arts venue is St James's Concert and Assembly Hall (www.stjames.gg), a church in College Street. Guernsey is not the place to go for nightlife, though it does have a few pubs with live music and a handful of nightclubs in St Peter Port. The Doghouse (www.doghouse.gg), located on Rohais, is the best venue in town for live entertainment, with live music most nights, plus monthly UK tribute bands. RED (www.red.gg) has a harbour view and a great list of cocktails.

Guernsey Aquarium

ACTIVITIES FOR CHILDREN

For a traditional family holiday, Guernsey has the ideal ingredients: acres of sandy beaches, crab-filled rock pools, myriad shells to collect and plenty of sporting activities. There's a great castle to explore (Castle Cornet, see page 28) and The Aquarium in St Peter Port. Sausmarez Manor in St Martin has two adventure play areas and a 9-hole pitch-and-putt golf attraction, Oatlands Village offers children's rides. On a rainy day you can take youngsters to the Beau Sejour Leisure Centre (www.beausejour.gg) on the hilltop above St Peter Port to enjoy the 25-metre indoor swimming pool and separate children's pool; also tennis and badminton courts and a crèche with activities for older children. Other places worth considering are the Folk and Costume Museum, with work sheets and prizes for children, and the Guernsey Museum, which has a Discovery Room for youngsters. The German Occupation and other World War II museums and fortifications may appeal to older children.

There aren't as many attractions on the smaller islands, but youngsters may fall in love with the islands' quaint ways. Because of the considerable walking or cycling involved and because of the inaccessibility of its beaches, Sark can be tough-going for small children. Herm, by contrast, where Shell Beach is just a 10-minute walk from the ferry, is a paradise for any short-legged adventurer.

CALENDAR OF EVENTS

For full listings go to www.visitguernsey.com/events.

Guernsey Heritage Festival End Mar–early May. More than 300 events take place across the islands.

Guernsey Literary Festival Second week in May. Four-day event featuring well known writers.

Alderney Performing Arts Festival May. Held over the late bank-holiday weekend, hosting concerts, shows, dances and workshops.

Liberation Day 9 May. Islanders celebrate the liberation from the German Occupying forces, which occurred on 9 May 1945.

Guernsey Seafood Festival 16–17 June. Celebrating the island's seafood.

Guernsey Floral Festival June. Nine days of tours, talks and workshops.

Alderney Food and Drink Festival: Late June–early July. The island's gastronomic highlight. Food foraging, zero-food-miles menus and local delicacies.

Guernsey in Bloom July. Celebrating the islands' flowers and gardens.

Town Carnival July. Fortnight with clowns, face painters and musicians.

Sark Sheep Racing July. Sheep, with teddy bears for jockeys, race over a set course.

Lé Viaer Marchi First Monday in July. Re-enactment of a 1900s market fair, with traditional music, dance and costume.

Torteval Scarecrow Festival Last weekend in July.

Rocquaine Regatta Early Aug. A day of entertainment, activities and fun on Guernsey's west coast.

Alderney Week Early Aug. Week-long carnival and community festival.

Fete d'Etai Mid-Aug. Medieval-themed entertainment at Castle Cornet.

The West Show Mid-Aug. Celebration of agricultural and horticultural traditions on the west coast.

The North Show Late Aug. Family entertainment including the Battle of Flowers with awards for the best floral floats.

Guernsey World Cuisine Festival End Aug–early Sept. Showcasing the best of the island's food through themed diners, guest chefs and more.

Tennerfest Oct–mid-Nov. Restaurants are packed out for six weeks when fixed menus start at £10 at 170 restaurants.

EATING OUT

Guernsey has a thriving gastronomic scene, particularly in St Peter Port. Eating out is an essential part of life on the island, and with its well-off residents, Guernsey has more than its fair share of up-market restaurants. Even the discerning French come across the Channel to indulge their palates. Annual culinary competitions testify to the islands' gastronomic pride and the islands hold regular food festivals and tasting events. For simpler tastes, there is no shortage of pizzerias, pubs with

⊙ THE GUERNSEY ORMER

If you happen to be on the island between January and April during spring tides, you might spot locals scouring the rocks in search of the near mythical gastropod: the ormer. This indigenous mollusc, related to the abalone, is found beneath rocks on the island's tidal sandbanks, and has a distinctive shell, well camouflaged from the outside but beautifully irridescent inside with a pearly rainbow sheen. Prized for its unique flavour, the ormer was once a staple of island dinner tables. Traditionally the shellfish were carried home in a basket, soaked, shelled, scrubbed, beaten with a steak hammer, browned in a frying pan, then cooked in a casserole with belly of pork, shallots and carrots. Overfishing led to the ormer becoming a gourmet rarity, and nowadays there are regulations to protect the stocks. Ormers can only be fished on specific days – generally those of the full moon, new moon and two days following, between January and April. They must be larger than 8cm (3in) and no breathing equipment, snorkel or diving suit is allowed during collection.

Fort Grey blue cheese

ploughman's lunches and beach kiosks where you can tuck into a tasty crab sandwich or a Guernsey cream tea.

Seafood is the speciality here and you'd be missing out if your visit didn't include at least one meal that had been harvested from the sea. The clear, warm waters around the island produce lobsters, prawns, scallops and crabs. Most of the island's small fishing boats return within 24 hours so the bulk of the fish sold is landed on the same day it is caught.

Given the proximity to France, it is not surprising that Gallic dishes feature on menus. Firm favourites are *moules marinières*, *moules-frites*, or *plateau de fruits de mer*. There are good farmhouse cheeses from Normandy and fresh French baguettes can be bought from bakers in St Peter Port (try, for example, Boulangerie Victor Hugo in Le Pollet). There are also plenty of places that cater for British tastes. You never have to go far to find a fry-up for breakfast, fish and chips or roast

Guernsey crab for sale

beef with Yorkshire pudding – the British institution of Sunday lunch is well-preserved.

SEAFOOD

Seafood features on virtually every menu. Your best bet is the fresh catch often chalked up on a blackboard outside restaurants. This will typically include mussels, scallops, shrimps and chancre crabs. Lobster is caught around the Guernsey shores and is served either cold with mayonnaise, Thermidor (braised in brandy or sherry and served in a creamy, mustard-flavoured sauce), or *à la nage*, in a white wine stock. Fish from Guernsey waters include sea bass, bream, brill, sole, grey mullet, monkfish, turbot and mackerel. Unless you choose a crab sandwich, seafood can be pricey. Fish is sometimes served by weight – ask roughly how much a dish will cost to avoid an unpleasant surprise at the end of the meal.

For a full blow-out, order a Breton-style *plateau de fruits de mer*, and work your way through a king-size banquet of oysters, scallops, crabs, mussels and lobster. The nicely plump chancre crab is the most widely available but the sweeter spider crab is more sought after.

LOCAL PRODUCE

The Channel Islands are famous for their herds of Jersey and Guernsey cows, with their doe eyes and concave faces. Symbolic of the islands, they feature on numerous souvenirs such as milk jugs and tea towels. The two islands jealously protect the purity of their own distinctive breed of cattle, which means that the milk tastes slightly different. Both breeds produce incomparably rich milk, and in the case of Guernsey's, it is high in beta carotine, giving it the lovely golden colour. Believed to have descended from two breeds of cattle from northern France, the Guernsey cow dates back to around 1700, and the purity of the breed has been guaranteed since 1789 when a ban was imposed on the import of live cattle to the islands. Today the Guernsey cows number less than 10,000 globally, and are on the watch list of the American Livestock Breeds Conservancy.

The Guernsey Dairy produces butter the colour of wild buttercups, cheese, ice cream and the renowned thick and golden Guernsey cream, often lavished on scones. It is also liberally spread on the traditional Guernsey *gâche*, a sweet bread made with raisins, sultanas and mixed peel, and pronounced 'gosh'.

Apart from Guernsey cows, the island's best-known export used to be tomatoes. These were introduced in 1865, eventually accounting for 75 percent of Guernsey's income. In more recent times cheaper Dutch imports have usurped 'Guernsey toms' from English shops, forcing the island's horticulturalists to switch their green houses to cut-flower production. Tomatoes are still grown for local consumption, along with celery, courgettes, peppers and most other salad ingredients. Potatoes are grown too,

Milk o'Punch Sunday

If you happen to be in Alderney on the first Sunday in May, between noon and 2pm, you'll be hailed with a free Milk o'Punch at any of the island's pubs. The punch is made from milk and egg, with a healthy tot of rum and some mystery ingredients.

Guernsey cream tea

but Guernsey dwellers will bend the knee to the deliciously earthy new potatoes grown by rival Jersey and likely to be found on the menu from March onwards.

The national dish is Guernsey Bean Jar, a variation of the French cassoulet. This hearty dish, comprised of various kinds of dried beans, plus pork, onions and herbs, is traditionally cooked overnight in a stone bean jar and served with crusty bread. There is also a Jersey Bean Jar and the island's emigrants in Canada are reputed to have inspired Mr Heinz's world-famous baked beans.

CIDER AND ALE

Cider was first introduced to the Channel Islands by the Normans and until relatively recently it was the main drink on the islands. In the 17th century it was given by farmers to their staff to make up their wages. Today cider afficionados can try the popular Rocquette Cider, made from locally-grown apples. But today the preferred tipple, as in the UK, is a pint of beer. The popularity of imported lager led to a sharp decline in the sales of local breweries. Randalls (www.randallsbrewery.com) established in St Peter Port in 1868, is the only one of the old breweries to survive and today they have a state-of-the-art brewery on St George's Esplanade. Pre-arranged group tours (minimum 12 people) take place on Friday evenings at 6–7.30pm. Visitors are shown how water, malt hops and yeast are converted into Breda Lager and Patois, Guernsey's only locally-brewed real ale. The only other brewery on the island is the White Rock microbrewery (www.whiterockbrewery.gg) which produces good quality craft beers with names like Wonky Donkey and Witch Hunter.

Cider and real ale fans head to Herm in June and September for the Ale and Cider festivals, hosted by the Mermaid Tavern. Held over six days, these are lively events with around 30 ales and a dozen ciders to try, and live music on some evenings. For information on dates and booking go to www.herm.com/events.

⊙ VRAIC

Vraic (pronounced 'rack' and Guernsey patois for seaweed) was for centuries gathered with horse and cart by St Peter's parishioners to enrich the crops. There are two types of vraic: the weed washed up on the beach after stormy weather and the type cut from the rocks, which was used as fuel by fishermen who could not afford coal or wood. Vraic collection days were party-like, with whole families gathered on the beaches, men wading out to the rocks on foot or going by boat, while women and children collected ormers, crabs and limpets in profusion. Spirits were kept high with vraic buns and cider, and at the end of the day the seaweed was brought up from the bay by horse and cart and families returned home to feast on shellfish. Cutting of vraic from the rocks was only allowed at certain times of year and was closely supervised by parish officials. Vraic days are sometimes held on the beach at L'Eree in celebration of the seaweed, featuring storytellers, foraging walks, cooking demonstrations, traditional stalls and children's activities.

WHERE TO EAT

You're rarely far from food on any of the islands. Almost every attraction and easily accessible beach has at least a café, there are snug pubs down many country lanes and hotels invariably woo non-residents with bar meals, gourmet menus and cream teas. You can choose from smart seafood restaurants, cosy bistros or seaside cafés, while a smattering of Italian, Portuguese, Chinese and Indian restaurants provide cosmopolitan touches. St Peter Port has by far the best choice and many of its excellent seafood restaurants have fine views of the harbour. The choice of restaurants is clearly more limited on the smaller islands although all three can offer you a slap-up meal.

Eating out at lunchtime, when many restaurants offer good value two-course set menus, is often cheaper than evening dining. Opening times are the same as those in the UK at lunchtime, but evening meals tend to be served earlier, especially at seaside restaurants where last orders are often at 8 or 8.30pm or even earlier. In summer it is usually wise to reserve a table in advance, especially if it's a warm evening and you want to dine alfresco.

Hedge Veg

As you travel around the island you'll see un-manned stalls selling home-grown fruit and veg, known locally as 'hedge veg'. You choose what you want – from cut flowers and new potatoes to courgettes and asparagus – then leave the correct change in an honesty box.

CULINARY EVENTS

Late autumn is the time for some real bargains, with dozens of restaurants, including many of the best, offering fixed-price menus from £10. The 'Tennerfest' lasts for six weeks from

October to mid-November and takes place throughout the Channel Islands. Over 170 eateries offer fixed price menus at heavily slashed prices. Menus are displayed in a special guide in *The Guernsey Press* (the island's daily newspaper) and on the website at www.tennerfest.com.

Hedge veg stall

The island hosts a variety of food events and festivals throughout the year. On certain Sundays from May to September St Peter Port seafront is closed to traffic and transformed by market stalls and alfresco dining. Visitors can take part in cookery demonstrations and free tasting of traditional dishes. The Taste Guernsey Food Festival takes the form of two events: in early September world cuisine is showcased on restaurant menus; while in June seafood takes centre stage. At the end of June virtually all of Alderney's restaurants take part in the Alderney Food and Drink Festival.

Country and farmers' markets throughout the island sell local produce. Among the best is the Saturday morning Farmers' market at Sausmarez Manor (see page 38) with a wide range of locally-made products and plants. You can experience Guernsey both on foot and with food on the Tasty Walks (see page 90). For up-to-date information on events, go to www.visitguernsey.com.

PLACES TO EAT

The price bands are based on a two-course meal with a glass of wine, excluding service charge.

££££	over £35
£££	£25–35
££	£20–25
£	under £20

ST PETER PORT

Da Nello's ££££ *46 Le Pollett, tel: 01481-721 552,* www.danello.gg; *lunch and dinner.* An Italian favoured by locals, with an attractive covered courtyard. Expect a warm welcome and a wide range of traditional pasta, seafood and meat dishes.

La Frégate ££££ *Les Cotils, tel: 01481-724 624,* www.lafregatehotel. com; *lunch and dinner.* Outstanding, quite formal hotel restaurant with magical views of the harbour and outer islands. The emphasis is on Guernsey seafood and fish, cooked with precision and artfully presented. The restaurant prides itself on its wines, 'which should enthrall and excite the connoisseur but not bamboozle the enthusiast'. Regarded by many as the best seafood restaurant on the island.

The Hook £££ *North Plantation, tel: 01481-701 373,* www.thehook.gg; *Tue–Sat lunch and dinner, Sun lunch.* Come for steak, seafood or sushi at this waterfront restaurant. If you fancy pushing the boat out, try half a Guernsey lobster in lime and chilli butter.

Mora £££ *The Quay, tel: 01481-715 053,* www.mora.gg; *lunch and dinner.* Spread over two floors, Mora offers fine views over the harbour. The busy ground-floor brasserie, serving tapas, gourmet burgers and shared platters, doubles as a cocktail bar. The more peaceful restaurant upstairs showcases the best of Guernsey's seafood.

Le Nautique £££ *Quay Steps, tel: 01481-721 714;* www.lenautiquerestaurant.co.uk; *Mon–Sat lunch and dinner.* One of Guernsey's top seafood restaurants, with lovely views over the marina if you're lucky enough to secure a window seat. Chef and owner Günter Botzenhart gives classical dishes a modern twist and his menu is constantly changing to make the most of produce in season.

Old Quarter Restaurant ££ *15 Mansell Street, tel: 01481-727 268,* www.oldquarter.co.uk; *Mon–Sat lunch and dinner, closed Mon lunch.* Set among cobbled streets, a warm welcome awaits you at this restaurant serving honest, no nonsense food with a slight Irish slant, in honour of the owner's roots.

Pavilion Brasserie £££ *St Pierre Park Hotel, tel: 01481-728 282,* www.thepavilion.co.gg; *lunch and dinner.* Chef Richard Bloomfield is a keen advocate of fresh Guernsey produce and fuss-free techniques, so expect dishes such as breaded Rocquaine Bay oysters and braised shanks of Sark lamb with red wine sauce. Dine in modern stylish surroundings or on a large terrace

Le Petit Bistro ££ *56 Lower Pollet, tel: 01481-725 055,* www.petitbistro.co.uk; *Tue–Sat lunch and dinner.* Authentic French cuisine in atmospheric bistro. Specialities feature *coq au vin*, *coquilles St Jacques* and frogs' legs. Excellent-value set lunches and early-bird dinners. The adjoining Le Petit Café serves lighter bites.

La Piazza ££ *Trinity Square, tel: 01481-725 085; Mon–Sat lunch and dinner.* This buzzing Italian offers some excellent-value meal deals, friendly attentive staff and seats outside in summer.

Pier 17 £££ *Albert Pier, tel: 01481-720 823,* www.pier17restaurant.com; *lunch and dinner.* One of the island's most popular restaurants with a stylish contemporary setting and great views over the working harbour and Castle Cornet. Book well in advance.

The Swan Inn £ *St Julian's Avenue, tel: 01481-728969, closed Sun and Mon.* This welcoming Victorian corner pub is a favourite for evening drinks and gastropub fare. Come for hearty helpings of home-made pies and burgers or the chef's weekly-changing dishes, such as house-smoked rack of lamb or line-caught Guernsey seabass with tapenade, garlic and almond cream. Meals are served both in the traditional downstairs bar or the stylish first-floor dining room.

AROUND THE ISLAND

Fermain Bay

Fermain Beach Café ££ *tel: 01481-238 636; opening times prone to change so telephone in advance; normally lunch daily, June–Aug also dinner daily.* This seafood café-cum-bistro is a great place to refuel after a bracing walk along the coast. Choose from Guernsey crab sandwiches, salmon ciabatta or mouth-watering cakes and enjoy the views of this lovely bay. The secluded location entails a fairly steep walk down the hill – but it is well worth it. You need to book well in advance for evening meals (high season only).

Jerbourg

The Auberge £££ *Jerbourg, St Martins, tel: 01481-238 485,* www.the auberge.gg; *closed Sun dinner.* Consistently excellent food in a modern, minimalistic setting opening on to a terrace with stunning views of neighbouring islands. The menu often features game such as venison and guinea fowl.

St Martin's

Bella Luce Hotel £££ *La Fosse, St Martin's, tel: 01481-238 764,* www.bellalucehotel.com; *lunch and dinner.* This is a stylish hotel in the peaceful green lanes of St Martin's, where you can come for light bar meals, a leisurely afternoon tea or gourmet Modern European cuisine. Head chef Simon McKenzie is passionate about local produce, and uses local fishermen and artisanal foodmakers. Bella's bistro opens out onto a lovely walled garden for summer meals.

La Barbarie Hotel £££ *Saint's Road, St Martin, tel: 01481-235 217, www. labarbariehotel.com; lunch and dinner.* This charming rural hotel is known for its cuisine. Come for creamy crab bisque, turbot in lobster sauce, pan-seared calves liver or slow-roast belly of pork.

Forest

Le Gouffre ££ *Le Gouffre, tel: 01481-264121; closed Mon, and Tue and Sun dinner.* This café/restaurant is the perfect spot for cliff-top walkers in need of respite: peaceful, with sunny terrace, (partial) sea views and excellent, freshly-prepared fare. Expect Mediterranean fish soup, salt and pepper squid, steaks and light lunches.

St Saviour

Auberge du Val £££ *Sous L'Église, St Saviours, tel: 01481-263 862, www. aubergeduvalguernsey.com; closed Mon, and Sun dinner.* Very popular traditional *auberge* in an attractive rural setting. Ideal for a simple bistro-style lunch or more adventurous evening meals.

The Farmhouse £££ *St Saviours, tel: 01481-264 181, www.thefarmhouse. gg; lunch and dinner.* In a hotel converted from an old farmhouse, the restaurant and bright, airy courtyard have a contemporary look and modern cuisine. Light lunches can be enjoyed by the outdoor pool in summer.

Mint Brasserie ££ *Le Gron, St Saviours (in the gardens of the Bruce Russell & Son Goldsmiths complex), tel: 01481-266 556, www.mint.gg; Tue–Sun lunch, Fri and Sat dinner.* This farmhouse-style brasserie-cum-tea room has won favour with its fair prices, home-made cakes and deserts, and à la carte lunches and dinners. The restaurant promotes locally-sourced seasonal ingredients where possible, and makes its own bean jar (see page 102).

Torteval

Imperial Hotel Restaurant ££ *Rocquaine Bay, Torteval, tel: 01481-264 044; lunch and dinner.* Sea views towards Fort Grey are the big attraction here. You can come any time for bar or main meals from the modern British menu or coffee in the gardens. The à la carte menu features seafood straight from the bay.

L'Erée

Taste of India £ *Sunset Cottage, L'Erée, tel: 01481-264 516, www.taste-ofindiaci.com; lunch and dinner.* Stroll across the beach then stoke up at this very popular Indian restaurant, just across from the bay, and enjoy the sunset. Takeaways are available.

Cobo Bay

Cobo Bay Hotel Restaurant, £££ *Cobo Bay Hotel, Cobo Bay, tel: 01481-257 102, www.cobobayhotel.com; lunch and dinner daily, closed for lunch in winter.* Spectacular sea views and sunsets are a big attraction here. The menu changes with the seasons, but you could start with diver-caught scallops and follow with monk fish or rib-eye steak. The restaurant has won awards for the quality of food and service.

Cobo Fish and Chip Bar £ *Cobo Coast Road, tel: 01481-254 276; Mon–Sat 11.30am–2pm and 4.30–9pm, Sun from 4pm (later at weekends and in high season).* Buy fish and chips from this basic but popular chippie and enjoy them while watching the glorious sunset over Cobo Bay across the road.

The Rockmount ££ *Cobo Coast Road, tel: 01481-252 778, www.therocky. gg; Mon–Sat lunch and dinner, Sun lunch only.* Family-friendly gastro pub with fabulous bay views and catering for all tastes. Along with pub favourites you'll find twice-baked Guernsey Cheddar soufflé, butternut squash and kale potato gnocchi, Rocquaine mussels or warm seabass Niçoise salad with soft quail eggs.

Castel

Fleur du Jardin ££ *Kings Mill, Castel, tel: 01481-257 996, www.fleurdu-jardin.com; lunch and dinner.* This country hotel serves some of the best gastro-pub fare in the Channel Islands. The emphasis is on local produce: superb locally-bred beef, line-caught seabass, west coast scallops or a locally-sourced crab sandwich.

Vale

The Beach House £ *Pembroke Bay, Vale, tel: 01481-246 494, www.beach-houseguernsey.com; June–Sept daily 9am–8pm, off-season Tue–Fri 11am–8pm, Sat–Sun 9am–8pm.* Right on the beach in a stark modern building, with a viewing gallery for meals above. Open for breakfast through to dinner, serving sandwiches, burgers and Pembroke fish and chips.

Surfside at Port Soif £ *Port Soif, Vale, daily 9.30am–6pm.* Excellent value home-made food including bacon butties, fresh crab sandwiches and generously-buttered Guernsey *gâche* (fruit loaf).

Roc Salt ££ *Mont Cuet Road, Chouet, Vale, tel: 01481-246 129, www.roc-salt.gg; Wed–Sat lunch and dinner, Sun 10am–4pm (maybe open additional days during peak times).* This is one of the best fish restaurants in the north of the island. Menus change regularly and dishes are simply cooked and flavoursome. Decor is shabby chic, and the balcony has fine views over Chouet Bay.

HERM

Conservatory Restaurant £££ *White House Hotel, Herm Harbour, tel: 01481-750 075, www.herm.com; usually daily for lunch and dinner end Apr–early Nov.* Traditional hotel restaurant where you can enjoy Guernsey seafood and lamb or full afternoon tea with uninterrupted sea views. Meals served on the lawn in fine weather. Extensive wine list, with many bought directly from Bordeaux châteaux.

Mermaid Tavern ££ *Herm Harbour, tel: 01481-750 050; www.herm.com; Apr–Oct lunch and dinner daily, restricted hours off-season; Grill Room Tue–Sat 5–9pm in season.* The social hub of the island, with pub lunches and a good choice of beers and wines. Steaks, fish and vegetarian dishes can be eaten out in the courtyard or inside the charming pub. The Mermaid is the venue of the occasional real ale and cider festivals.

The Ship Inn Brasserie ££ *White House Hotel, Herm Harbour, tel: 01481-750 075; www.herm.com; Apr–end Sep daily from 9am.* Serving excellent cuisine from the kitchens of The White House Hotel, the Ship Inn has a more informal atmosphere than the Conservatory Restaurant. Come for a fry-up breakfast, seafood or sandwich lunches, cake and cream teas or full dinners with good-value wines. Meals can be taken alfresco on the patio, in the bar by the log fire or in the restaurant.

SARK

La Sablonnerie ££££ *Little Sark, tel: 01481-832 061, www.sablonnerie-sark.com; lunch and dinner mid-Apr–late Oct.* Located on peaceful Little Sark this is the perfect place to stop on a walking or cycling tour. You can enjoy snacks, cream teas and seafood platters in the flower-filled tea gardens or a lunch based on the ingredients produced on the hotel's organic farm. For guests at this charming old farmhouse, or others staying in Sark, there are candlelit dinners. Roasted sea scallops, lobster Thermidor or fillet of home-grown beef can be followed by crème brûlée with a montage of exotic fruits and berries.

Stocks ££££ *tel: 01481-832 001, www.stockshotel.com; lunch and dinner.* Fine dining in elegant surrounds. Choose from à la carte, *table d'hôte*, lobster or bistro menus and make the most of the fruits of Sark's seas: mackerel, seabass, turbot and hand-dived scallops. Lobsters are caught within a three-mile radius of the hotel and normally require 24 hours' notice.

ALDERNEY

Braye Beach Hotel Brasserie £££ *Braye Street, tel: 01481-824 300, www.brayebeach.com; lunch noon–2pm, dinner 6–8pm (until 9pm during summer).* Book a table overlooking the lovely Braye beach and tuck into turbot with pan-seared scallops, shellfish bisque or butter-poached lobster. The hotel is rated four-star so prices are higher than average.

Braye Chippie £ *Braye Harbour, tel: 01481-823 475; Wed–Sat 5–8pm, with extended hours in high season.* Very popular chippie, with plenty of seating inside and out, right by the harbour. Bring your own bottle.

Bumps Bar & Bistro ££ *Victoria Street, St Anne, tel: 01481-823 197; lunch and dinner daily, except Sun dinner off-season.* A long-standing favourite among islanders for superb seafood, along with steaks and vegetarian options. The chef is also the owner, which is always good news. Service is attentive and friendly, and there's a sunny patio for alfresco dining.

Cantina Number 6 ££ *6 Braye Street, tel: 01481-824 063; Tue–Sat lunch and dinner.* Come to this buzzing bistro-type place for a really pleasant variation on the normal pub/restaurant setting. The menu mostly consists of tasty tapas plates, both large and small. A specials board adds to the already extensive and varied choice.

Georgian House ££ *Victoria Street, St Anne, tel: 01481-822 471, www. georgianalderney.com; lunch and dinner.* This family-run hotel restaurant has a lovely sheltered garden at the rear. The menu is a mix of traditional English pub and European cuisine, with emphasis on seafood, and use of local and sustainable produce where possible. Very friendly staff.

Jack's Brasserie £ *Victoria Street, tel: 01481-823 933; Mon–Sat 9am–4pm, with extended hours in high season.* This is a popular spot for breakfasts, light lunches, and coffee and cakes. With a sunny terrace on the High Street, it's a good spot to relax and watch the world go by.

Le Pesked ££ *30 Victoria Street, tel: 01481-823 841; lunch and dinner.* Distinctly French flavours are delivered with skill at this delightful restaurant set in the cobbled streets off St Annes. Run by Brittany chef David Ollivrin, his classic French cooking is given a modern twist and will not disappoint. The three-course set menu is excellent value. Book ahead.

A–Z TRAVEL TIPS

A SUMMARY OF PRACTICAL INFORMATION

A

ACCOMMODATION

From simple B&Bs to stylishly converted farmhouses and chic boutique hotels, Guernsey offers accommodation to cater for most tastes. But while places to stay are plentiful you won't find many bargains. The best deals tend to be packages that include air or sea transport. Many of the hotels offer this option on their websites; alternatively you can do it through specialist operators. For example, Channel Islands Direct (www.channelislandsdirect.co.uk) or FlyGuernsey (www.flyguernsey.com) offer deals whereby the total cost for a week's holiday in a hotel, travel included (and sometimes car hire), is less than the cost of accommodation alone booked through the hotel. Rates are almost invariably cheaper off-season and there are some great deals at the hotels that remain open in winter. For rooms in July and August book well ahead. Supplements are usually charged for sea view rooms, although it's often worth the extra for the fabulous view you wake up to.

Old-fashioned values are still often adhered to, but that doesn't mean you won't get Wi-fi or power showers in the upper bracket hotels. Guernsey has one five-star hotel, the Old Government House Hotel & Spa, and some of the four-star hotels have undergone stylish revamps. **Self-catering** is increasingly popular, whether in seaside apartments or country cottages. For utter isolation Fort Clonque (see page 140) on Alderney sleeps up to 13 and can be rented from the Landmark Trust.

For details of accommodation on all the islands visit the relevant tourist office website (see page 130).

As a base, St Peter Port offers the best sightseeing, shopping and dining options. Buses from here will take you all over the island; it is also convenient for hopping across to Herm or Sark. But wherever you stay on the island you are never far from the capital.

AIRPORTS

Guernsey Airport (tel: 01481-237 766; www.guernsey-airport.gov.gg)

is located in the parish of Forest, 3 miles (5km) southwest of St Peter Port. Arrival at the small airport is normally stress-free with quick luggage pick-up, customs and passport control, and a taxi rank and bus stop right outside. The airport is on several regular bus routes including nos. 62/71/95, which all take you to the St Peter Port bus terminus. Tickets can be bought on the bus. A taxi from the airport to St Peter Port costs from around £16–18 depending on the location of your hotel. Rental cars can be picked up at the airport.

Tiny Alderney Airport is just over a mile from St Anne. Aurigny (www.aurignynew.com) is the main airline for the island. Taxis meet arriving planes and rental cars can be booked.

B

BICYCLE RENTAL

Guernsey's hills are quite surmountable for any cyclist who is reasonably fit, but if you haven't biked for 20 years it's probably not the place to restart. You can feel very surrounded by cars at times and it can be a tight squeeze passing larger vehicles on tiny lanes. The most peaceful roads are the Ruettes Tranquilles (Quiet Lanes) which together form a network across the parishes of Castel, Forest, St Andrew, St Martin, St Sampson, St Savour and the Vale. These signposted lanes have a speed limit of 15mph (24kmh), though not all motorists adhere to the limit. There are coastal paths suitable for cyclists along the west coast and a 2-mile (3km) cycle path on the sea side of St Peter Port with great views of cruise ships and neighbouring islands. Cycling is not permitted on nature trails or along the cliff paths in the south of the island. Guernsey Tourist Information in St Peter Port provides a useful little guide, free of charge, with 11 island routes ranging from 7 to 12 miles (11 to 19km).

On car-free **Sark** pedal power is the preferred means of transport and you should keep to the left despite the absence of cars. You can't miss the bike-hire shops on Mermaid Lane and along The Avenue. In high season book in advance. On **Alderney** the size of the island and its peaceful lanes make it ideal for cycling. Cycles can be hired by the harbour in Braye and in Victoria Street, St Anne. Visitors are forbidden to cycle on **Herm**.

Those travelling to Guernsey on Condor Ferries can bring bikes to the island free of charge.

Bikes can be hired from:

GUERNSEY

Donkey's Days Out, Houmet Lane, Vale (tel: 07781-433 611; www.donkeysdaysout.co.uk). Bikes for hire and themed guided bike tours of 2–4 hours, visiting sites of historical and natural interest.

Millard & Co, 9–11 Victoria Street, St Peter Port (tel: 01481-720 777; www.millards.org).

Go Guernsey Cycle Hire, North Plantation, St Peter Port (tel: 07781-103 692; www.go-guernsey.gg).

SARK

A and B Cycles, Mermaid Lane (tel: 01481-832 844; www.atobcycles. com**).**

Avenue Cycle Hire, The Avenue (tel: 01481-832 102; www.avenuecyclessark.co.uk).

ALDERNEY

Auto-Motion, Braye Harbour (tel: 01481-823 352 or 07781-142 655; www.automotionalderney.com).

Cycle and Surf, St Anne (tel: 01481-822 286 or 07781-154 045; www.cycleandsurf.co.uk).

BUDGETING FOR YOUR TRIP

Costs of flights from the UK to Guernsey vary hugely from around £80 to £400 return, depending on the airline, time of year and day of the week (weekends are usually more expensive). Return flights from London Gatwick or Southampton to Guernsey with Aurigny cost from around £110 per person. In high season the Condor ferry from Poole to Guernsey costs £300–500 return for a family of four with a car. A three-star hotel charges £10–200 for a double room, a luxury hotel £200–300. Restaurant and bar prices are similar or slightly higher than those in the UK. Most attractions are free for young children. Museum admissions for adults range from £4 to £10. A taxi from the airport to St Peter Port costs £16–18.

C

CAMPING

Guernsey has three attractive and peaceful campsites: the centrally located Fauxquets Valley Farm Camping Site (www.fauxquets.co.uk) which was AA Campsite of the Year 2015 for South West England; La Bailloterie Camping (www.campinginguernsey.com) in a rural setting in the north and Vaugrat Camping (www.vaugratcampsite.com), a short walk from the northwest beaches. Alderney's Saye Bay site (www.sayebeachcamping.co.uk) lies directly behind the north coast's sandy bays. Of Sark's two basic sites, La Valette (www.sercq.com) is dramatically located near the cliffs. The island of Herm has a simple, well-run campsite (www.herm-island.com/camping).

CAR HIRE

Car hire prices are similar to those in the UK, fuel is slightly cheaper. A valid driving licence is required with no endorsements for dangerous or drunken driving in the last five years. Drivers must have held a full licence for a year and must be over 20 or 21 (sometimes 25) years of age, depending on the company. There are also varying maximum age restrictions. Car hire companies in Guernsey are plentiful and there is little difference in price between the international and local companies. Expect to pay around £160 for a week's rental of a small car, with an extra £5 a day if you hire a satnav. All rented cars are branded with a large letter H on the number plate.

GUERNSEY
Europcar (tel: 01481-239 511; www.europcarguernsey.com)
Hertz (tel: 0800 735 1014; www.hertzci.com)

Value Rent a Car (agents for Avis; tel: 01481-243 547; www.valueren-tacar.co.uk).
Rhino Car Hire (tel: 0845-508 9845; www.rhinocarhire.com).
ALDERNEY
Braye Hire Cars (tel: 01481-823 881; www.brayehirecars.com).

CLIMATE

The Channel Islands have the highest average number of sunshine hours in the British Isles, although the summer temperatures are no higher than those in some parts of southern England. As in the UK, the best months to go are from May to September, the hottest months being July and August. High temperatures in mid-summer are tempered by sea breezes.

The sea temperatures are refreshing for swimming, averaging 62.8°F (17.1°C) in summer. The Channel Islands have one of the largest tidal movements in the world.

The following chart gives the average maximum temperature for St Peter Port, Guernsey:

	J	F	M	A	M	J	J	A	S	O	N	D
°C	8	9	10	11	14	17	19	20	18	15	11	10
°F	47	49	50	52	58	62	67	67	64	59	52	49

CLOTHING

The climate is similar to that of the southern part of the UK so take a couple of sweaters and a rainproof jacket even in mid-summer. Otherwise T-shirts and shorts/skirts should suffice, not forgetting a sunhat, sunglasses and sun cream – the sun's rays can be deceptively strong. One of the best ways of seeing the islands is on foot so a stout pair of shoes is useful. Topless bathing is generally accepted, though far from widespread, and baring all on the island is inappropriate. Shopping in a swimsuit in St Peter Port is best avoided, too. Some nightclubs ban jeans and trainers.

CRIME AND SAFETY

Guernsey is a safe place for a holiday but it is worth taking all the usual precautions: always lock car doors and don't leave your valuables unattended. Dial 999 for police, fire, ambulance or coastal rescue services. Report a loss or theft to the police within 24 hours if an insurance claim is to be made.

D

DRIVING

Many roads are very narrow, with high hedges or granite walls and visibility can be poor. The lanes are used by tractors, cyclists, pedestrians, as well as buses and cars, so be aware of your surroundings. Signposting is poor, some satnavs don't work and it is easy to lose your way, although on such a small island it's unlikely you will be lost for long.

Given the narrow lanes and the maximum speed limit of 35mph (55kmh) (and a good deal less in towns and along the Ruettes Tranquilles or Quiet Lanes that have a limit of 15mph/24kmh) there is no point in bringing or hiring a turbo-charged car. Touring caravans are not permitted entry but a limited number of motorhomes can be accommodated on the three authorised camp sites on the island. A motorhome permit, which should be obtained in advance from the campsite, must be available for inspection by the ferry operator and the Guernsey Border Agency.

Rules of the Road The rules reflect those of the UK: driving is on the left, seat belts are compulsory for adult front seat passengers, children must wear belts or a suitable child/infant restraint in both front and rear seats; it is an offence to hold a mobile phone whilst driving. Fixed alcohol limits and roadside breath testing are similar to the UK. Police can and do make random checks and penalties are severe.

A wide yellow line across the junction of a minor road means stop and give way to traffic on the major road. A yellow arrow on the road warns of a junction ahead; a single yellow line along the roadside means that vehicles cannot park or wait at any time. Many junctions on Guernsey have a filter-in-turn system, marked by a cross-hatched yellow box painted on the road. You must not enter the box until your exit is clear.

Parking Most on-street parking and car parks in main shopping areas require a parking clock to indicate your time of arrival. Some rental companies leave the clock in the car, if not ask them to supply one. Alternatively they can be purchased from the Driving & Vehicle Licensing Office (Bulwer Avenue), Guernsey Information Centre, garages and from some newsagents. Although you have to pay for the card (£2.75) the actual parking is free. If you have just arrived and have a GB number plate, a note in the window of the time you arrive at the car park will suffice.

Most of the parking near the centre of St Peter Port is short stay (two or three hours). The major town car parks are on the Harbour piers, the largest being the North Beach area where two- and three- hour parking is nearly always available. There is no park-and-ride service, but if you are going to be in town for longer than three hours, or if you are going on a day trip to one of the neighbouring islands, there are several convenient 10-hour car parks. A bit further out, there are various options (up to 23-hour), although these do fill up early.

E

ELECTRICITY

The current is the same as that of the UK, 240 volts AC, with British-style three-pin sockets. Visitors from other European countries will need an adapter; those from the US will also need a transformer.

EMBASSIES AND HIGH COMMISSIONS

Australia Australian High Commission, Australia House, The Strand, London WC2B 4LA; tel: 020-7379 4334; www.uk.embassy.gov.au.

Canada Canada High Commission, Canada House, Trafalgar Square, London SW1Y 5BJ; tel: 020-7004 6000; www.canadainternational.gc.ca.

New Zealand New Zealand High Commission, New Zealand House, 80 Haymarket, London SW1Y 4TQ; tel: 020-7930 8422; www.nzembassy. com.

Republic of Ireland Irish Embassy, 17 Grosvenor Place, London SW1X 7HR; tel: 020-7235 2171; www.embassyofireland.co.uk.

South Africa South Africa High Commission, South Africa House, Trafalgar Square, London WC2N 5DP; tel: 020-7451 7299; www.south africahouseuk.com.

United States US Embassy, 33 Nine Elms Lane, London SW11 7US; tel: 020-7499 9000; www.usembassy.gov.

EMERGENCIES

Dial 999 for police, fire, ambulance or coastal rescue services. The Princess Elizabeth Hospital, at Rue Mignot, St Andrews, GY6 8TW (tel: 01481-725 241) has a 24-hour emergency unit. There is no reciprocal health agreement between Guernsey and the UK and hospital treatment is charged for, with a very limited number of ex-emptions. Primary Comprehensive medical insurance is therefore strongly recommended.

Herm has no medical facilities, though helicopter-borne emergen-cy services are available. The Sark Medical Practice (tel: 01481-832 045; www.medical.sark.gg) has a drop-in surgery Mon–Sat 9–10am, a booked surgery from 4–5pm (except Wed and Sat) and an out-of-hours emergency service. For serious cases patients can be transferred, usually by the St John Ambulance boat, to the Princess Elizabeth Hospital in Guernsey. Alderney has the small Mignot Memorial Hos-pital (tel: 01481-822 822) and The Island Medical Centre at Le Val (tel: 01481-822 077).

Road accidents involving personal injury or serious damage must be reported to the police within 24 hours. Minor accidents not involv-ing injury need not be reported provided the names and addresses of those concerned are exchanged. If in doubt contact the island police on 01481-725 111.

G

GAY AND LESBIAN TRAVELLERS

Guernsey only decriminalised homosexuality in 1983, but today the general attitude of islanders towards gays is not so different from that in the UK. Same-sex marriage or partnerships have been officially recognised on Guernsey and Alderney since 2017 but are still under discussion on Sark. Liberate (www.liberate.gg) is a Guernsey charity which aims to include, inform and support the LGBTQ (Lesbian, Gay, Bisexual, Transgender and Questioning) communities across the Channel Islands.

GETTING THERE

Year-round air and sea packages, short breaks, flights and accommodation can all be arranged through specialist tour operators. For details see www.visitguernsey.com.

From the UK

By air. All visitors flying to the Channel Islands need a passport or photo ID. Regular year-round flights operate from airports throughout the UK (but not Heathrow), with added services in high season. Flights take 40 minutes from London Gatwick and as little as 30 minutes from some regional airports. **Flybe** (tel: 0371-700 2000; www.flybe.com) flies direct to Guernsey from Birmingham, Norwich, Exeter, Southampton and other UK regional airports. **Aurigny** (tel: 01481-267 267; www.aurigny. com) flies to Guernsey from Gatwick, Stansted, Manchester, East Midlands, Leeds Bradford, Bristol and Southampton. Although the low-cost airlines have brought down the prices of getting to Guernsey the airport charges are high and real bargains are hard to come by. The cheapest fares are normally secured by booking well in advance on the internet and avoiding weekends and the busiest times of year. Aurigny and

Waves (www.flywaves.gg) provide an island-hopping service between Jersey, Alderney and Guernsey.

From the US, Canada, Australia, New Zealand and South Africa, the most efficient route is via London Gatwick, from which frequent daily flights serve Guernsey.

By sea. The only ferry line from the UK to Guernsey is **Condor Ferries** (tel: 0845-609 1026; www.condorferries.com) who operate services all year round. The state-of-the-art trimaran, 'Liberation', accommodating up to 880 passengers and 245 cars, departs from Poole and takes three hours to Guernsey. It is not uncommon for boats to be cancelled or delayed because of the weather conditions, particularly off-season. Facilities include a cafeteria, several bars, a soft play area for children and a duty-free shop with some excellent deals, especially on alcohol. Club-class seating is available, with reclining seats and, for an extra charge, steward service.

Condor Ferries also operate a slower service from Portsmouth on the conventional Clipper car/passenger ferry. The return crossing is overnight with the option of one-, two-, three- or four-berth cabins and en-suite facilities. Fast ferry services to Guernsey from Jersey and St Malo in France are also operated by Condor Ferries.

From Guernsey, it is a 20-minute ferry hop to Herm and 50 minutes to Sark; Jersey and Alderney are each a 20-minute flight away; Jersey is one hour by sea, Alderney 1 hour and 25 minutes.

Visitors bringing their own car must have an insurance certificate, the complete vehicle registration document and a valid driving licence or International Driving Permit. Bikes can be taken across on Condor ferries free of charge.

Package holidays. The islands' tourist information offices provide details of UK tour operators with Channel Islands programmes. Tour companies specialising in Guernsey include Premier Holidays (tel: 0844-493 7531, www.premierholidays.co.uk/guernsey), Channel Islands Direct (tel: 0800-640 9058, www.channelislandsdirect.co.uk) and Guernsey Travel (tel: 01534-496 660 , www.guernseytravel.com).

Overseas visitors should contact the British Tourist Authority in their own country (www.visitbritain.com).

GUIDES AND TOURS

Island Coachways (tel: 01481-720 210; www.icw.gg) offer twice-weekly guided coach tours around the island in summer and also offer Heritage and Occupation tours. Guernsey Taxi Tours (tel: 07781-111 999; www.guernseytaxitours.gg) offer individual around-the-island tours that allow you to stop and take photographs.

Walking tours. Guernsey has around 20 accredited guides offering walks to suit all abilities and interests. These include walks to wild and windswept Lihou Island, hidden green lanes, Victor Hugo's House, guided photo tours taking in the most scenic viewpoints of Guernsey, and walking tours of Herm and Alderney. For full details go to www.guernseyguidedtours.com or visit the Guernsey Information Centre in St Peter Port.

H

HEALTH AND MEDICAL CARE

There is no reciprocal health agreement between Guernsey and the UK and apart from treatment solely within Guernsey's A&E department visitors have to pay for medical services and treatment. This includes emergency hospital treatments (such as operations) not within A&E, repatriation and out-patient appointments. Doctors and dentists are in private practice and all patients are required to pay for treatment and prescriptions. UK visitors are therefore advised to take out comprehensive health insurance or check that their existing policy covers travel to the island. Australia and New Zealand have reciprocal care agreements with Guernsey which cover emergency hospital treatment.

The Princess Elizabeth Hospital, (Rue Mignot, St Andrews, GY6 8TW; tel: 01481-725 241) has a 24-hour emergency unit. The majority of GP surgeries provide a service for visitors. The Guernsey Information

Centre can provide details of island surgeries, alternatively a list of doctors is available at post offices, or ask your hotel. Medical prescriptions can be dispensed at any of the island pharmacies. Boots has an outlet on the High Street in St Peter Port and provides a full range of over-the-counter and prescription medicines.

Tap water is perfectly safe to drink.

L

LANGUAGE

English is spoken throughout all the Channel Islands. Some older citizens may communicate in Jèrriais, Guernésiais and Sercquiais – the local patois based on Norman French – in Jersey, Guernsey and Sark respectively, but you're more likely to come across Portuguese being spoken by seasonal workers. Most road, street and place names (and surnames) can be traced to Norman French, although they often receive anglicised pronunciation; some street names are bilingual, with the traditional French version appearing alongside the contemporary English name (not a translation).

M

MAPS

You can pick up a free up-to-date Perry's map of the island, which also includes Herm, Sark and Alderney, at the Guernsey Information Office in St Peter Port, also at the bus station, at hotels and many other outlets. The Information Office also has free detailed maps of St Peter Port. For more detail you can purchase *Perry's Guide*, a booklet of road maps with every little lane. A useful and widely available walking map of the island (free of charge) includes suggested walks, with details of walking time, terrain, points of interest and refreshment stops. If you are walking your way around the islands you might also consider the Ordnance Survey-style map of the Bailiwick of Guernsey, with Guernsey at 1:15000, and Alderney, Herm and Sark on the reverse at 1:10000.

MEDIA

All English national newspapers and some European ones arrive in the early morning on the day of publication, weather permitting. *The Guernsey Press* is the island's daily newspaper. The annual *Essential Guernsey Guide*, covering island attractions, eating out and shopping, can be picked up free of charge from the tourist information centre and other outlets. UK national radio and television stations are broadcast in Guernsey and there is a local ITV contractor – Channel Television. There are two local radio stations: BBC Radio Guernsey and the commercial station Island FM.

MONEY

English sterling is freely accepted on the islands, as are all major debit and credit cards. Guernsey also has its own currency, in the same denominations as UK notes and coins, apart from the fact that it still has £1 notes. UK and Guernsey currency can be used within the islands but Channel Island sterling may not be accepted in the UK apart from in banks, which will exchange notes. Some shops will accept euros, normally only in note form, and change will generally be given in sterling. All major debit and credit cards are widely accepted throughout the islands. ATM machines can be found at all of the high street banks in St Peter Port, the airport, some supermarkets, garages and out-of-town banks throughout the island. Sark has no ATMs.

The absence of VAT on the islands and the low duty on imported luxury items is mainly offset by the higher transport costs.

OPENING HOURS

Banks. Banks have similar opening hours to those in the UK, with some open on Saturday morning.

Shops. Normal opening times are Mon–Sat 9am–5.30pm. There is no general Sunday opening in Guernsey but some shops in St Peter Port and a few convenience food stores and small supermarkets remain open, especially when a cruise ship arrives.

Tourist attractions. Most museums and tourist attractions are open from April to October from 10am to 5pm, though the times are subject to change and some of the major sites are open all year. For a list of current openings go to the Visit Guernsey website (www.visitguernsey. com).

Pubs. Guernsey licensing hours are Mon–Sat 10am–12.45am, Sun noon–12.45am.

P

POLICE

In an emergency dial 999, for non-emergency calls dial 01481-725 111. The police headquarters are located at Hospital Lane, St Peter Port, GY1 2QN (see also Crime and Safety on page 120).

POST OFFICES

Guernsey runs its own post office and issues its own stamps. Mail leaving Guernsey, Sark or Herm must bear Guernsey postage; from Alderney, both Alderney and Guernsey stamps can be used. Unlike in the UK mail is not divided into first and second class and note that Guernsey's pillar boxes are normally blue, rather than red. The main post office in Smith Street, St Peter Port, is open Monday to Friday 8.30am–5pm, Saturday 8.30am–noon. Channel Island stamps are much in demand by collectors worldwide and the main post office has a philatelic display and stamp sales.

PUBLIC HOLIDAYS

Guernsey has the same public holidays as the UK with an additional day's holiday on 9 May, Liberation Day, commemorating the end of the

German Occupation in 1945.

1 January New Year's Day
March or April Good Friday and Easter Monday
First and last Monday in May Spring Bank Holidays
9 May Liberation Day
Last Monday in August August Bank Holiday
25 December Christmas Day
26 December Boxing Day

T

TELEPHONES

The code for Guernsey, Herm, Sark and Alderney is 01481 from the UK and +44 1481 internationally. STD codes for the UK from Guernsey are the same as those used from the UK. Although the code appears to be a UK one, the Channel Islands are excluded from the UK national price rates and the costs of calls are similar to those for Europe. Mobile networks, provided by Cable & Wireless, JT, Sure and Airtel Vodafone, require a roaming facility plus international dialling codes. 'Pay as you go' phones only operate in Guernsey where there is an agreement with the network provider. Check with your provider if in doubt. Coin-operated payphones are located around the island.

TIME ZONES

As in the rest of the UK, the Channel Islands are on Greenwich Mean Time (GMT), with clocks moving forward in late March, and reverting back in late October.

New York	**Guernsey**	Paris	Jo'burg	Sydney	Auckland
7am	**noon**	1pm	2pm	11pm	1am

TIPPING

Hotels and restaurants often add a service charge (10–15 percent) to the bill, in which case there is no need to tip. If service has not been satisfactory, this charge may be deducted from the bill. If the charge has not been added to the bill, 10 percent is an average tip for satisfactory service.

Taxi drivers and hairdressers do not include service charges; a tip of 10 percent is normal for satisfactory service.

TOILETS

There are clean public toilets at main sites and at most beaches. Cafés are usually laid back about the public using their facilities, although if you buy a drink it will be appreciated.

TOURIST INFORMATION

The Guernsey Information Centre (North Esplanade, St Peter Port, tel: 01481-723 552; www.visitguernsey.com; open Mon–Sat 9am–5pm, Sun 10am–1pm, reduced hours in winter) has a wealth of information on the island, including guided walks, exhibitions, theatre bookings and accommodation details. Various free booklets are available on *what to see and do in Guernsey, Herm, Sark and Alderney* and *cycle tours and walks in Guernsey*.

Sark has an information centre on The Avenue (tel: 01481-832 345; www.sark.co.uk). Alderney has a Visitor Information Centre with some excellent walking guides at 51 Victoria Street, St Anne (tel: 01481-822 333; www.visitalderney.com).

TRANSPORT

Guernsey has a variety of transport options, both public and private. The smaller islands, however, leave you with little choice between a bicycle and your own two feet.

Buses. Guernsey's bus service is operated by CT Plus on behalf of the Environment Department. The network services most parts of the island including the main beaches and visitor attractions. Information including routes, fares and timetables can be accessed on www.buses. gg; alternatively information is available from the bus terminal or Visitor Information Centre. A single fare of £1 applies to all journeys including the round island tour. Travel passes are available for one, two and seven days for individuals and families (up to three children under 17 travelling together).

Since many bus stops are served by several routes you are advised to wave down the relevant bus as it approaches. You can also hail a bus and the driver will stop to pick you up provided it is safe to do so (but not in St Peter Port, Bridge or the St Sampson area).

Several companies operate scheduled or tailor-made bus tours, including Island Coachways (tel: 01481-720 210; www.icw.gg) and Intransit (tel: 01481-245 845; www.intransit.gg).

Taxis. Guernsey has licensed taxis at three ranks: in central St Peter Port and St Sampson (on the bridge), and at the airport. Pre-booking is advisable whenever possible. Taxi companies include: A+S Taxis (tel: 07781-125 544), Island Taxis (tel: 01481-700 500) and Panza Taxis (tel: 07781-111 340).

Carriages (Sark). Horse-drawn carriages on Sark seat six or ten people and normally do one-hour tours in the north of Sark or two-hour tours of the north and south. All tours start and finish at La Collinette, the crossroads at the top of the Harbour Hill.

Inter-island Ferries and France

Herm: Travel Trident (tel: 01481-721 379; www.traveltrident.com) operates ferries from St Peter Port to Herm roughly every hour July to August, with fewer boats during off-peak times. Go early to avoid the day-trippers in the summer. The journey time is 20 minutes.

Sark: The Isle of Sark Shipping Company (tel: 01481-724 059; www. sarkshippingcompany.com) runs day trips to Sark with generally five ferries a day in summer. The journey time is around 50 minutes.

Alderney: the fastest though not the cheapest way to visit the island of Alderney from Guernsey is to take the 20-minute flight operated by

Aurigny (see page 123). Ferry passenger services from Guernsey to Alderney are very limited but talks are in progress to provide a scheduled inter-island ferry.

Day trips to Jersey and France: Condor Ferries (www.condorferries. com) operate day trips from St Peter Port to Jersey and to St Malo in France. Manche Îles Express (tel: 01481-701 316; www.manche-iles. com) operate passenger ferries connecting Guernsey with Jersey, and Carteret, Diélette and Granville in Normandy.

TRAVELLERS WITH DISABILITIES

With all its steps and steep streets, especially in St Peter Port, Guernsey is not ideal for travellers with disabilities. For information on accessibility on the island go to www.disabledgo.com, which can be used in conjunction with the Visit Guernsey website (www.visitguernsey.com).

On-street parking and public car parks have designated areas for UK and EU blue parking card holders. Guernsey has 'low-floor' buses that are designed to carry disabled passengers. For more information go to www.buses.gg. For wheelchair-accessible taxis contact the Guernsey Information Centre or go to www.visitguernsey.com.

For equipment hire contact the Health Care Equipment Centre (tel: 01481-729 268).

The Radar National Key Scheme, which enables disabled people to access locked public toilets, operates in Guernsey. Visitors are advised to bring their own key; alternatively they are available from the Guernsey Information Centre.

For four-wheel mobility scooters on carless Sark, contact Sark Tourism (tel: 01481-832 345; email: office@sark.co.uk).

V

VISAS AND ENTRY REQUIREMENTS

Guernsey has the same passport and visa requirements as the UK. Although a passport is therefore not necessary for visitors arriving from the UK, airline passengers will need valid photographic ID in order to travel, and a passport is required if you visit France.

As Guernsey is not a full member of the EU, you can still purchase duty-free goods when travelling to and from the island. Maximum allowances are 200 cigarettes or 100 cigarillos or 50 cigars or 250 grams of tobacco; 4 litres of still table wine and 1 litre of spirits or strong liqueurs over 22 percent volume or two litres of fortified wine, sparkling wine or other liqueurs; 16 litres of beer or cider; £390-worth of other goods (watches, jewellery, perfume, cameras, etc).

W

WEBSITES AND INTERNET ACCESS

Many hotels offer Wi-fi, sometimes chargeable. Free Wi-fi hotspots include Guernsey Airport, Guernsey Harbour, Guernsey Visitor Centre, the Guille-Allès Library and a few cafés and pubs.

Here are some useful websites:

www.visitguernsey.com Official Guernsey website

www.sark.co.uk Official Sark website

www.visitalderney.com Official Alderney website

www.herm.com Official Herm website

www.islandlife.org This is the largest community website serving the Channel Islands. Full of information about the islands, although not always up-to-date.

www.buses.gg Everything you need to know about the Guernsey buses.

www.guernseypress.com Online version of *The Guernsey Press*, for daily news, information on what's on, tide times and more.

www.guernseytickets.gg Event ticket sales.

RECOMMENDED HOTELS

The choice of accommodation ranges from luxury boutique hotels to simple B&Bs. Self-catering is now very popular, with a choice of over 60 cottages, bungalows or apartments on offer, well suited to those who want to enjoy the island at their own pace, and in their own space. Some offer shared leisure amenities (sometimes with an adjoining hotel), such as swimming pool children's play area and activity options.

The Guernsey Tourism website (www.visitguernsey.com) has a comprehensive section on accommodation. For hotels and self-catering on Herm, Sark and Alderney, visit www.herm.com, www.sark.co.uk and www.visitalderney.com respectively.

Most places will require deposit or credit card details before confirming a reservation, and for special deals you may need to pay in full prior to arrival. VAT is not chargeable in the Channel Islands. Prices fluctuate according to the season, with some great deals in winter. Prices are generally at least as high, if not higher, than the UK, but substantial savings can be made by booking accommodation and travel together as part of a package (see page 115).

Reservations for a holiday in July and August need to be made well in advance. The shoulder months of March, April, May, September and October are, weather permitting, good times of year to travel to Guernsey as rates are lower and accommodation is easier to find. In hotels with restaurants half-board terms are normally available.

Accommodation is rated from one to five stars. Gold and silver accolades are awarded to hotels and self-catering units that consistently deliver service and hospitality above what is required by the star rating.

The price bands below are a guideline for the cost of a standard double room and breakfast for two people in high season.

££££	over £220
£££	£170–220
££	£130–170
£	under £130

ST PETER PORT

Best Western Hotel de Havelet £££ *Havelet, St Peter Port, tel: 01481-722 199,* www.dehaveletguernsey.com. A Georgian house, 15 minutes' walk uphill from St Peter Port (or courtesy minibus in summer) with fine views of the harbour and islands. Indoor pool with sauna, steam room and Jacuzzi.

La Collinette ££ *St Jacques, St Peter Port, tel: 01481-710 331,* www.la-collinette.com. This welcoming family-run hotel with cottages and apartments has a big sheltered garden and pool. It is a 10-minute walk downhill to St Peter Port, through the Candie Gardens. Contemporary restaurant and bar.

La Frégate Hotel £££ *Les Cotils, St Peter Port, tel: 01481-724 624,* www.lafregatehotel.com. Stylish, boutique hotel in its own grounds in St Peter Port, blending the charm of an 18th-century manor house with the amenities of a modern hotel. Fantastic views across the islands and arguably the best restaurant in Guernsey (see page 106).

Duke of Richmond Hotel £££ *Cambridge Park, St Peter Port, tel: 01481-726 221,* www.dukeofrichmond.com. This popular four-star hotel beside the Candie Gardens has a contemporary look with its black and white lounge and bar/restaurant leopardskin fabrics. Guest room prices vary substantially depending on views (many overlook the sea) and the degree of luxury – there's a Penthouse and four Junior suites.

Fermain Valley £££ *St Peter Port, tel: 01481-235 666,* www.fermainvalley.com. Used for business as well as pleasure this four-star hotel has stunning sea views and is only a 5-minute drive from St Peter Port (traffic permitting). There are five categories of stylish rooms, spread over two separate buildings. A walk down the valley brings you to one of the prettiest bays in Guernsey.

The Old Government House Hotel and Spa ££££ *St Ann's Place, St Peter Port, tel: 01481-724 921,* www.theoghotel.com. The former official residence of Guernsey's governor, the OGH (as it's familiarly known) dates from 1858 and retains many original features. This is the only five-star hotel on the island. Expect plush individually designed bedrooms, top-notch cuisine in the Brasserie or Curry Room, traditional afternoon teas and excellent service. Leisure facilities include a well-equipped spa, gym and outdoor heated pool.

St Pierre Park, Spa and Golf Resort ££ *St Peter Port, tel: 01481-728 282, www.handpickedhotels.co.uk/stpierrepark*. Luxurious but slightly imper-sonal modern hotel set in 35 acres of parkland on the outskirts of St Peter Port. Ideal for sports enthusiasts with a 9-hole golf course, ten-nis courts, indoor pool, health club and spa. The various eating options include the Pavilion Brasserie (see page 107).

AROUND THE ISLAND
St Martin

Bella Luce Hotel ££ *La Fosse, St Martin, tel: 01481-238 764, www.bella lucehotel.com*. This ancient manor house has been transformed into a luxury boutique hotel, one of the most desirable on the island. Down a leafy lane amid lush gardens, it offers opulent guest rooms, some with four-poster beds, a candlelit-restaurant with top quality cuisine, a cellar bar where gin is distilled and a spa.

La Barbarie ££ *Saints Bay Road, St Martin, tel: 01481-235 271, www.labarbariehotel.com*. The combination of friendly and attentive staff, good food and comfortable, well-equipped guest rooms make this one of Guernsey's most appealing three-star hotels. It's worth paying a bit extra for the 'superior' category rooms which have the space and facilities of a four-star hotel. The location, tucked away in the narrow lanes of St Martin, provides easy access to the cliffs and coves of the south coast.

Hotel La Michele £ *Les Hubits de Bas, St Martin, tel: 01481-238 065, www.lamichelehotel.com*. This small family-run hotel, renowned for hospi-tality, has its own restaurant and a secluded garden with an attractive heated swimming pool.

La Trelade ££ *Forest Road, St Martin, tel: 01481-235 454*, www.latrelade-hotel.co.uk. Set back from the road in its own gardens the hotel is only half a mile from Guernsey's scenic south coast with its cliff top walks; it's also close to the main bus routes. Good leisure facilities include health suite with indoor pool and gym.

St Saviour

Auberge du Val £ *Sous L'Eglise, St Saviour, tel: 01481-263 862*, www.aubergeduvalguernsey.com. Set in 3 acres (1.2 hectares) of an idyllic valley, this welcoming old farmhouse has a popular restaurant (closed Sun evening and all day Mon) serving fresh food, with herbs and vegetables from the garden. The nine guest rooms all have en-suite bathrooms.

The Farmhouse £££ *Route des Bas Courtils, St Saviour, tel: 01481-264 181*, www.thefarmhouse.gg. Run by the Nussbaumer family for three generations, this four-star boutique hotel is one of Guernsey's favourite places to stay. The 14 bedrooms are furnished in contemporary style, with large walk-in showers. Dependent on the season, the popular restaurant offers meals available by the fire, poolside or in one of the gazebos. Room rates include car hire.

Castel

Cobo Bay Hotel ££ *Coast Road, Cobo, Castel, tel: 01481-257 102*, www.cobobayhotel.com. Ideal beach holiday hotel with good- value rooms across the road from Cobo Bay. The award-winning restaurant, renowned for seafood, has a spacious terrace with unparalleled sea and sunset views. Small complimentary health suite.

Fauxquets Valley Campsite £ *Candie Road, Castel, tel: 01481-255 460*, www.fauxquets.co.uk. Wonderful campsite in a tranquil valley. Excellent amenities include heated pool, restaurant and bar, shop and children's playground and games room.

Fleur du Jardin ££ *Kings Mills, Castel, tel: 01481-257 996*, www.fleurdu-jardin.com. Named after a breed of Guernsey cow, this old farmhouse has been stylishly renovated and offers rooms with bleached timber walls and sandstone wet rooms. First-class gastro-pub food, a solar-heated pool and a health suite.

Hougue du Pommier ££ *Route Hougue du Pommier, Castel, tel: 01481-256 531,* www.channelhotels.com/hotel-hougue-de-pommier. Creeper-covered old farmhouse converted and extended into a welcoming inn with a variety of rooms. Cosy communal areas put the emphasis on food: traditional dishes at the Tudor Bar, an à la carte menu in the restaurant and cream teas in the sun lounge. Eight-acre (three-hectare) garden with a pretty pool.

La Roche Guest House £ *Rohais de Haut, Castel, tel: 01481-258 088,* www.larocheguesthouseguernsey.com. A charming Georgian home in peaceful grounds in the centre of the island, this is one of Guernsey's loveliest guest houses. The hospitable owners are accredited tour guides and are happy to help guests with their itineraries on Guernsey and to neighbouring islands. They are excellent cooks too, providing copious breakfasts and evening meals on request. You can enjoy these under the vines in the conservatory, beside the kitchen aga, in the dining room with open fire or, in summer, by the outdoor heated spa pool.

Torteval

Clifftop Cottages *Le Petit Manoir, Route de Pleinmont, tel: 01481-263 090,* www.clifftopcottages.com. Five self-catering cottages sleeping between 2 and 7 in a peaceful, rural part of the island close to stunning cliff walks. Private patio areas with garden furniture. Available year-round; £400-£800 per week depending on size and season.

Vale

The Bay Apartments *Vale, tel: 07781-145 129,* www.thebayguernsey. co.uk. Four spacious, self-catering apartments, three with spectacular views of sandy Pembroke Bay. Facilities include tennis, outdoor swimming pool and health and beauty salon. Convenient for golfers with L'Ancresse Golf Club nearby. £550–1,500 per week depending on size and season.

Peninsula Hotel ££ *Les Dicqs, Vale, tel: 01481-248 400,* www.peninsula hotelguernsey.com. This 99-room hotel overlooks Grand Havre Bay and its extensive, landscaped gardens have direct access to the beach. Atmosphere is a bit impersonal, but facilities are plentiful, particularly for families, with outdoor and children's pool, playground, volleyball and table tennis.

HERM

White House Hotel £££ *Herm, tel: 01481-750 000,* www.herm.com; *closed off-season.* In a harbour-side setting, this is an ideal place to unwind away from the 21st century (no TVs or iPod docking stations here). It has been family-run for over half a century and the emphasis is on old-fashioned values, good service and culinary excellence. Amenities include a solar-heated swimming pool, a tennis court, a croquet lawn – or books and board games when the weather is inclement. Cottages are also available.

SARK

La Sablonnerie ££££ *Little Sark, tel: 01481-832 061,* www.sablonnerie-sark.com; *closed off-season.* Located on Little Sark, this remote farmhouse hotel is reached by the owner's horse-drawn carriages and offers rural tranquillity with secluded cottage garden and croquet lawn. Most guests dine here and make the most of the excellent cuisine (see page 112). One of the loveliest hotels on the Channel Islands providing a total escape.

Stocks Hotel ££££ *Sark, tel: 01481-832 001,* www.stockshotel.com. A family-owned country house in the wooded valley leading to Dixcart Bay. The Dame of Sark used to entertain royalty here and an escape tunnel survives from the days of the German Occupation when officers, including the Commandant, were billeted here. Comfortable guest rooms come with free Wi-Fi. Menus feature home-made and local produce (see page 112).

Sue's B&B £ *Cae de Met, Sark, tel: 01481-832 107; closed Jan–Easter,* www.suebnb.com. Sue Guille owns and runs this wonderful B&B with three garden-and-sea-view en-suite guest rooms, and one smaller room. Breakfast is taken on the sunny veranda or in the beautiful garden. Sue's husband George operates boat trips around the island.

ALDERNEY

Braye Beach Hotel ££-£££, *Braye Street, Alderney, tel: 0800-280 0550 (UK freephone)*, *www.brayebeach.com*. Chic designer hotel with a perfect setting overlooking Braye Beach. There are four categories of bedrooms – all are light and bright and have free Wi-fi. Book ahead for sea-view rooms as they are popular and fill up quick. Other facilities include a 19-seat cinema and four options for eating and drinking.

Farm Court £ *Le Petit Val, Alderney, tel: 01481-822 075*, *www.farmcourt-alderney.co.uk*. This good-value B&B, in a collection of small converted barns set around an enclosed cobbled courtyard, is run by a friendly husband-and-wife team who prepare generous breakfasts. A self-catering cottage that sleeps three is also available.

Fort Clonque *Alderney (book through the Landmark Trust, tel: 01628-825 925, www.landmarktrust.org.uk)*. Built in the 1840s, Fort Clonque has been converted by the Landmark Trust into self-catering accommodation, with sleeping quarters for up to 13 people (or 14 if you count the ghost!), in four different buildings. Being cut off from Alderney at high tide, it suits those with a sense of adventure. Four nights from £763.

INDEX

GUERNSEY

INSIGHT ◉ GUIDES POCKET GUIDE

First Edition 2018

Editor: Tom Fleming
Author: Susie Boulton
Head of DTP and Pre-Press: Rebeka Davies
Picture Editor: Tom Smyth
Cartography Update: Carte
Update Production: Apa Digital
Photography Credits: Alamy 4MC, 5T, Anna Mockford & Nick Bonetti/Apa Publications 4TC, 4ML, 5TC, 5M, 5MC, 6L, 6R, 7, 7R, 11, 12, 15, 16, 19, 21, 24, 27, 29, 30, 33, 34, 37, 39, 40, 42, 43, 44, 45, 47, 49, 50, 53, 55, 56, 58, 60, 63, 64, 66, 67, 69, 70, 72, 74, 76, 78, 80, 82, 84, 86, 88, 90, 92, 93, 95, 96, 99, 100, 102, 105, AWL Images 1, iStock 4TL, 5M, Robert Harding World Imagery SMC
Cover Picture: Shutterstock

Contact us

Every effort has been made to provide accurate information in this publication, but changes are inevitable. The publisher cannot be responsible for any resulting loss, inconvenience or injury. We would appreciate it if readers would call our attention to any errors or outdated information. We also welcome your suggestions; please contact us at: hello@insightguides.com
www.insightguides.com

Distribution

UK, Ireland and Europe: Apa Publications (UK) Ltd; sales@insightguides.com
United States and Canada: Ingram Publisher Services; ips@ingramcontent.com
Australia and New Zealand: Woodslane; info@woodslane.com.au
Southeast Asia: Apa Publications (SN) Pte; singaporeoffice@insightguides.com
Worldwide: Apa Publications (UK) Ltd; sales@insightguides.com

Special Sales, Content Licensing and CoPublishing

Insight Guides can be purchased in bulk quantities at discounted prices. We can create special editions, personalised jackets and corporate imprints tailored to your needs. sales@insightguides.com; www.insightguides.biz

© 2018 Apa Digital (CH) AG and Apa Publications (UK) Ltd